Vasco da Gama

RICHARD WORTH

GREAT EXPLORERS

Jacques Cartier

James Cook

Hernán Cortés

Sir Francis Drake

Vasco da Gama

Sir Edmund Hillary

Robert de La Salle

Lewis and Clark

Ferdinand Magellan

Sir Ernest Shackleton

GREAT EXPLORERS

Vasco
da Gama

RICHARD WORTH

CHELSEA HOUSE
PUBLISHERS
An imprint of Infobase Publishing

GREAT EXPLORERS: VASCO DA GAMA

Chelsea House
An imprint of Infobase Publishing
132 West 31st Street
New York NY 10001

Library of Congress Cataloging-in-Publication Data
Worth, Richard.
  Vasco da Gama / Richard Worth.
    p. cm. — (Great explorers)
  Includes bibliographical references and index.
  ISBN 978-1-60413-423-0 (hardcover)
  1. Gama, Vasco da, 1469-1524—Juvenile literature. 2. Explorers—Portugal—Biography—Juvenile literature. 3. India—Discovery and exploration—Portuguese—Juvenile literature. 4. Discoveries in geography—Portuguese—Juvenile literature. I. Title. II. Series.
  G286.G2W676 2008
  915.4'04245092—dc22
    [B]   2009014163

Chelsea House books are available at special discounts when purchased in bulk quantities for businesses, associations, institutions, or sales promotions. Please call our Special Sales Department in New York at (212) 967-8800 or (800) 322-8755.

You can find Chelsea House on the World Wide Web at
http://www.chelseahouse.com

Series design by Lina Farinella
Cover design by Keith Trego

Printed in the United States of America

Bang EJB 10 9 8 7 6 5 4 3 2 1

This book is printed on acid-free paper.

All links and Web addresses were checked and verified to be correct at the time of publication. Because of the dynamic nature of the Web, some addresses and links may have changed since publication and may no longer be valid.

CONTENTS

A Passage
to India

IN JULY 1497, FOUR SAILING SHIPS GLIDED OUT OF THE
crowded harbor at Lisbon, capital of Portugal, located on the
Tagus River. The small flotilla was under the command of an
experienced sailor, Captain-Major Vasco da Gama. He had
not been the first choice of Portuguese king Manuel I to lead
this expedition. In fact, that honor had gone to his father—
Estâvão da Gama, one of Portugal's leading military commanders. But he had died suddenly and his son Vasco had
taken over the command. Da Gama had met the king near
Evora in Portugal and taken an oath of allegiance before set-
ting off on his expedition.

On July 8, wrote historian K.G. Jayne in his book *Vasco
da Gama and His Successors, 1460 to 1580,* the men "started
in solemn procession for the place of embarkation, Vasco
and his officers leading the way, with lighted candles in their
hands, while a body of priests . . . followed. . . . A vast con-
course had assembled on the mud-flats which then lined the

Portuguese explorer Vasco da Gama commanded one of the first ships to reach India from Europe by sea route. Da Gama's route around the Cape of Good Hope is still followed by sailing vessels today. He proved that the Indian Ocean was not a landlocked sea as Europeans had believed, and was later rewarded with the titles Dom and Admiral of the Sea.

estuary [river] . . . the whole multitude fell on their knees in silence," while one of the priests led them in prayer and blessed their voyage. Then the men were rowed out from the docks to their ships.

As the ships headed out into the Atlantic, their white sails with blood red crosses billowed in the wind. The entire expedition carried a crew of about 170 men. Before the voyage, the men had been carefully trained in skills such as rope-making, carpentry, and plank-making. These were essential to make repairs on the ships during the many weeks at sea. Vasco da Gama sailed aboard one of the ships, the *São Gabriel*, while his brother Paulo commanded the *São Rafael*. Each of these ships was probably about 100 to 120 tons, 75 feet long, and about 25 feet wide. They were low in the center with high castles on the bow and stern, and armed with cannon. Each of the ships carried three sails—a square foresail in front, a mainsail in the center, as well as a triangular lateen sail in the rear. In addition to the larger ships, there was a smaller caravel commanded by Nicolau Coelho and a storage ship with supplies for the voyage, captained by Concalo Nunes.

Even the largest of the vessels, the *São Gabriel* and the *São Rafael*, were tiny in comparison to large sailing ships that would ply the seas several centuries later. The sailors on board them were undertaking a dangerous journey that would last many weeks in the Atlantic Ocean where they would be buffeted by heavy seas and even stronger storms. No one knew if he would ever return because the squadron was headed on a journey that no European had ever taken.

They were hoping to sail south through the Atlantic, round the tip of Africa, and then travel northward to India. Da Gama's mission was twofold. He was hoping to spread Christianity from Portugal to other parts of the world. He also wanted to open up a lucrative trade in spices between Portugal and India. Spices like pepper and cinnamon were grown in India and they were greatly in demand throughout Europe to flavor food. If the Portuguese merchants could control the spice trade, they could greatly enrich their nation.

Only 10 years earlier another Portuguese adventurer, Bartolomeu Dias, had journeyed as far as the southern end of Africa. He had traveled in small caravels. Dias realized that he could have turned his ships northward and continued to India. But his men had been at sea long enough, and he decided to turn back, returning to Portugal.

The Voyage to Africa and India

For the longer voyage to India, Dias had designed the two larger ships that made up da Gama's expedition. This time, he only planned to go part of the way with da Gama—to the Cape Verde Islands off the north coast of Africa, which had been colonized by the Portuguese. During this first leg of the voyage, a dense fog engulfed the ships. The *São Raphael* became separated from the rest of the expedition and only rejoined the other ships at the Cape Verde Islands in late July. From there, da Gama planned to make a large westward loop into the Atlantic Ocean. In this way, his sailing vessels might pick up favorable winds that would blow him south and then eastward toward southern Africa.

Da Gama relied on a compass to guide his voyage. He also had an astrolabe—a device that could be used to measure the angle of the sun or the position of the North Star above the horizon and determine the latitude. The mariner's astrolabe was a heavy metal ring with degrees marked out around the outside. Attached to the center was a metal pointer called an alidade, which could move across the ring. A sailor held the astrolabe toward the sun and pointed the alidade directly toward it to determine its angle as marked on the ring. From this information, using charts, the sailor could determine the current latitude of the ship, that is, the distance north or south of the equator.

In addition to charting their course at sea, life aboard ship for the sailors involved constant work. They had to pump out water that might seep into the holds of the ships, constantly pull in or let out the sails to make sure they could take full advantage of the wind, and check the cargo. Food aboard ship included a daily ration of dried biscuits, beef or pork, water, and wine. After many days at sea, the biscuits turned moldy and the meat became rotten.

When they weren't working, the crew probably tried to get what little sleep they could as the ships tossed on the waves. Since the vessels were small, there were very few places to lie down for even a few hours of rest. Storms may have interrupted their sleep, and the sailors prayed regularly that they might be saved from the terrors of being at sea for so many days out of sight of land.

When the Portuguese squadron had come within 600 miles of the east coast of South America, they picked up the westerly winds that guided them back to Africa. Eventually, one of the sailors who had been assigned to the crow's nest on top of a ship's mast, yelled down that he had sighted land. Da Gama reached St. Helena Bay on the south coast of Africa in November. "[W]e cast anchor in this bay," the ship's log recorded, "and we remained there eight days, cleaning the ships, mending the sails and taking in wood." By the time the crew put in at St. Helena Bay, they had not seen any land for 4,500 miles—much longer than any other European sailors, even those who had sailed with Christopher Columbus to the New World in 1492.

Da Gama described the natives he saw there as "tawny-colored. Their food is confined to the flesh of seals, whales and gazelles, and the roots of herbs. They are dressed in skins. . . . They are armed with poles of olive wood to which a horn, browned in the fire, is attached." One of the crew, named Fernão Velloso, accompanied the natives to their village where they ate a dinner of seal meat roasted over a fire. Somehow a misunderstanding developed, and Velloso was forced to flee from the natives and return to the ships.

The expedition then headed southward toward the Cape of Good Hope. At first, because of the winds, they were unable to round the cape. But the winds changed and they were able to continue their journey, eventually putting into shore at Mossel Bay, located east of the cape. Here they encountered local tribesmen who agreed to give them an ox in return for some red caps and bells that the Portuguese carried as trade goods. The ox provided a fresh supply of meat for the men. Before leaving, the Portuguese played trumpets and danced in their ships, while the tribesmen accompanied them onshore to the sound of flutes and dancing.

By Christmas 1497, da Gama had reached the southeast coast of Africa, which he called Natal—after the Nativity or birth of Jesus Christ. Portugal was a Christian country, and da Gama not only wanted to control the spice trade, he also hoped to spread Christianity along the coast of Africa and across India. His ships dropped anchor along the Limpopo River, which he called the River of Copper because the native people he saw there wore copper bracelets and necklaces.

From this location, the squadron headed northward along Africa's west coast, where Muslim merchants had already established lucrative trading ports. One of these was located on the Bazaruta Islands—a center of pearl fishing—and another was at Sofala, where gold was shipped after being dug from mines farther inland. In March 1498, the Portuguese squadron arrived at the Muslim city-state of Mozambique, an island on the coast with houses built from white stone.

The Muslim merchants were hostile toward the Portuguese, fearing that they had come to compete with them for trade. Nevertheless, da Gama was permitted to visit with the sheikh who governed Mozambique and attempted to bargain with him for supplies. The sheikh, after seeing that the Portuguese did not carry gold, silver, or ivory, refused to deal with them. Da Gama left the city, but then returned and tried to

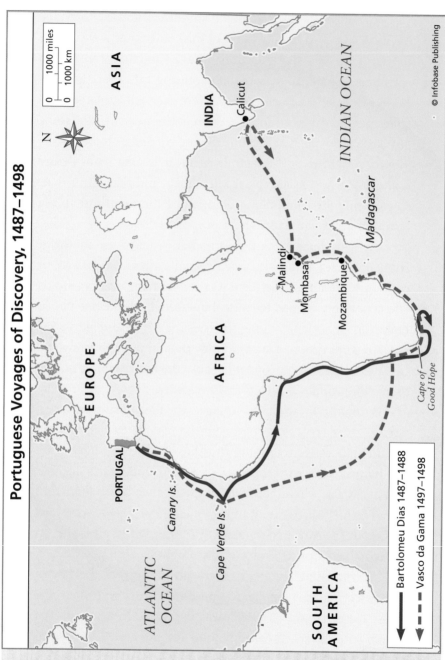

Portuguese Voyages of Discovery, 1487–1498

ASIA

INDIA

Calicut

INDIAN OCEAN

© Infobase Publishing

0   1000 miles
0   1000 km

N

EUROPE

AFRICA

Malindi
Mombasa
Mozambique

Madagascar

PORTUGAL

Canary Is.

Cape Verde Is.

Cape of
Good Hope

ATLANTIC
OCEAN

SOUTH
AMERICA

Bartolomeu Dias 1487–1488
Vasco da Gama 1497–1498

Encouraged by the discoveries of Christopher Columbus, the Portuguese were determined to reach the Indies before the Spanish to take advantage of the wealth. Bartolomeu Dias was the first to round the Cape of Good Hope, opening up a sea route from Europe to East Asia. Da Gama went even further, sailing into waters previously unknown to European vessels.

force the townspeople to give him water. When they refused, he bombarded Mozambique with his artillery and eventually obtained a supply of water for his men.

From Mozambique, da Gama sailed northward to Mombassa, reaching this city in early April. When the townspeople learned that da Gama and his men were Christians, they refused to deal with him. Instead they tried to attack his ships at night but were driven off. A short distance northward, however, da Gama arrived at the port city of Malindi. The local ruler, or rajah, was involved in a conflict with the sultan of Mombassa and welcomed da Gama as a possible ally in his struggle. In return for a few trade goods, he presented the Portuguese with a supply of sheep and even agreed to go out and visit their ships. According to K.G. Jayne, "[H]e was rowed out to the ships, royally attired in a damask robe trimmed with green satin, and an embroidered turban. His dignity required the support of two cushioned chairs of bronze; a crimson satin umbrella protected him from the sun, and a band discoursed more or less sweet music on various kinds of trumpets, including two that were fashioned of ivory and were as large as the musicians who performed on them."

At Malindi, da Gama not only received fresh supplies, he was also given a knowledgeable Arab pilot. The pilot understood the winds and currents of the Arabian Sea and would help the Portuguese reach India. With his help, da Gama continued his journey across the Arabian Sea, reaching Calicut on the Malabar Coast of India on May 20, 1498. The voyage had taken more than 10 months to complete.

Calicut was a lucrative center of the spice trade—the goal of the Portuguese sailors. It was the end of their voyage, but also the beginning of a new era that would change the history of the world.

The Rise
of Portugal

PORTUGAL IS A LONG, NARROW COUNTRY THAT LIES ON THE western coast of Europe along the Atlantic Ocean. With approximately 500 miles (800 kilometers) of coastline, Portugal occupies part of the Iberian Peninsula along with Spain, which is much larger. Broad rivers cut across Portugal, emptying into the Atlantic, including the Douro in the north, where the port of Oporto is located, the Tagus in central Portugal where Lisbon lies, and the Sado located farther south. During the fifteenth century, Lisbon was the largest city with a population of about 40,000 while about 8,000 people lived in Oporto.

Long before this period, about 1000 B.C., a group of tribes known as the Lusitani had begun arriving in Portugal, establishing farms and building fishing villages along the coast. They went out into the Atlantic Ocean in small boats to catch fish. When the Romans invaded in the second century, the Lusitani tried to prevent them from conquering the area. They were led by a brilliant general named Virianthus. After

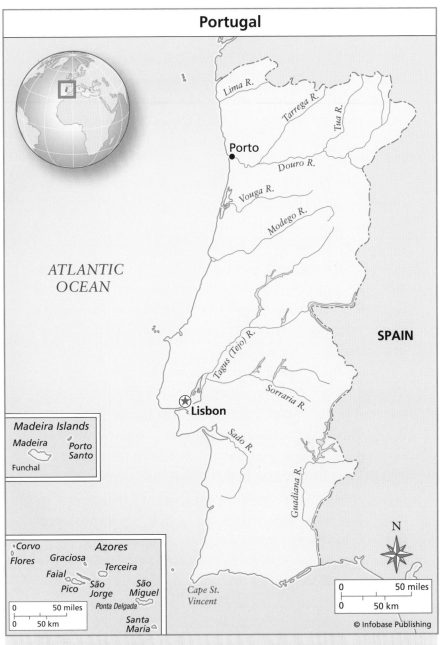

Portugal

ATLANTIC OCEAN

Lima R.

Tarrega R.

Tua R.

Porto

Douro R.

Vouga R.

Modego R.

SPAIN

Tagus (Tejo) R.

Sorraria R.

Lisbon

Sado R.

Guadiana R.

Cape St. Vincent

Madeira Islands

Madeira   Porto Santo

Funchal

Corvo
Flores   Graciosa   **Azores**
              Terceira
Faial
Pico   São   São
        Jorge   Miguel
Ponta Delgada
              Santa
              Maria

0   50 miles
0   50 km

N

0   50 miles
0   50 km

© Infobase Publishing

Portugal's location on the west coast of the Iberian Peninsula was an advantage during the sixteenth century, when the economies of northern Europe were dependent on maritime trade. The port cities of Lisbon and Oporto (or Porto) became the commercial centers of the country. Although Portugal lacked the wealth and population of its rivals, it would lead the European community in the exploration of sea routes to Africa, Asia, South America, and the Atlantic islands.

he was assassinated in 140 B.C., the Romans wore down the resistance of the Lusitani and took control of the land that they called Lusitania. The Roman conquerors developed a large port at Lisbon, built new cities, connected them with paved roads, and constructed bridges over the large rivers. They also raised fine thoroughbred horses on estates along the Tagus River, planted vineyards and olive groves, and worked rich gold and copper mines.

By the fifth century A.D., Roman power had greatly declined around the Mediterranean world. In place of the worldly kingdom of Rome, a spiritual kingdom of Christianity had begun to rise. Founded in the first century A.D., it had spread across Europe and as far west as Lusitania. Early in the fifth century, the Visigoths—a group of Germanic tribes—conquered the Iberian Peninsula. Many of them were Christians, and the northern Portuguese city of Braga became an important center of Christianity on the peninsula.

Soon the power of Christianity was facing a strong challenge from a new religion—Islam. Founded by the Prophet Muhammad in the seventh century A.D, Islam grew quickly after the Prophet's death in 632. His followers, known as Muslims, led large armies that conquered vast areas of the present-day Middle East. In 711, they invaded Iberia and eventually overcame the defenses of the Christian cities in Portugal. In 756, the Muslim leader Abd al-Rahman I set up a new kingdom at Córdoba, located in present-day southern Spain.

The Muslims created a brilliant civilization in Iberia that would endure for several centuries. As historian David Birmingham wrote in *A Concise History of Portugal*, "Science and learning were among the most profound contributions which Muslim scholars brought to Portugal." They translated the philosophy and mathematics of the ancient Greeks. The Muslims improved navigation by bringing the astrolabe and compass to Portugal and developing more advanced methods of ship-building. "The greatest economic impact of Muslim culture," according to Birmingham, "was felt in agriculture. Irrigation was improved and extended as huge water wheels were built to lift water from the rivers to the fields." The Muslims also introduced new architectural styles, especially in their religious centers called mosques, as well as music and dancing.

The Reconquest

Although most of the Iberian Peninsula was controlled by the Muslims, small Christian kingdoms still managed to maintain a foothold in the north. Little by little, Christian armies pushed southward, raiding Muslim strongholds around Braga in the northwest. With the help of armed knights from France, the Christians expanded their control as far south as Oporto on the Douro River in the eleventh century. This area, which was known as Portugal, was ruled by Henry, a nobleman from Burgundy (part of present-day France). Henry, who was called the count of Portugal, had married the daughter of King Afonso VI of Castile, part of present-day Spain. Afonso claimed control of Portugal.

After Henry's death in 1112, his son, Afonso Henriques, eventually became the count of Portugal. He continued to enlarge the territory under his control, defeating the Muslims at the Battle of Ourique in 1139. Although greatly outnumbered, Afonso still managed to win a convincing victory that safeguarded his kingdom. After the Battle of Ourique, instead of considering himself a count, Afonso now began calling himself king of the independent Kingdom of Portugal. He pushed the borders of his new kingdom farther southward, eventually conquering Lisbon in 1147. Castile, however, refused to recognize the independence of Portugal. Afonso was forced to carry on a series of military campaigns to defend his new kingdom.

After King Afonso's death in 1185, Portugal was firmly in control of the land around the Tagus. Over the next century,

The battle of Aljubarrota (August 14, 1385), commanded by the armies of King John I of Castile and King John I of Portugal, brought about the defeat of Castile. In addition, Portugal gained its independence and a new dynasty, the House of Aviz, was established. In the painting depicting the battle of Aljubarrota, the victorious Portuguese are on the right.

Portuguese armies continued to push down the peninsula capturing the Muslim strongholds on the southern end, known as the Algarve. This area, however, was also claimed by Castile, which led to continuing conflicts between the Portuguese and the Castilians during the next 100 years. In 1297, hostilities came to an end when a peace treaty was signed between Portugal and the reunited kingdoms of Castile and León. Ferdinand IV of Castile married Constance, the daughter of King Denis of Portugal, while Afonso, son of Denis, married Beatrice, daughter of Ferdinand IV.

The foreign policy of King Denis and his successors achieved its objective to preserve the peace between the

BATTLE OF ALJUBARROTA

Considered one of the decisive battles in Portuguese history, Aljubarrota was fought in central Portugal on August 14, 1385. The Portuguese army was commanded by General Nuno Álvares Pereira, a veteran of the wars against Castile. His army included mounted knights, archers carrying crossbows, and infantry on foot—about 9,000 soldiers. Still, they were greatly outnumbered by the Castilian forces, under the command of King John I of Castile. The Castilians totaled 30,000 to 40,000 men, including French cavalry who were allied with Castile. In addition, the army included many Portuguese nobles who supported King John's claim to the throne.

The Portuguese took up a defensive position on a hill, forming a square that was made up of dismounted cavalry holding lances. On each side of the square were archers, who could fire arrows at the enemy from two directions as they approached the Portuguese position. Behind the square were other ranks of soldiers under the command of King John, whose mission was to prevent the Castilians from coming in and attacking the Portuguese from the rear. In front of the square, the Portuguese may have also dug ditches to disrupt the charging Castilian cavalry, while on the flanks were small streams and hillsides.

As the French cavalry charged, they were struck by wave after wave of arrows from the archers, knocking many of the mounted knights off their horses. They were followed by the Castilian infantry, pushing forward under a hail of arrows. Although they greatly outnumbered the Portuguese, the Castilians were forced to maneuver within the small space between the streams and hillsides on the flanks. Nevertheless, they managed to reach the Portuguese square and engage in heavy hand-to-hand combat. By this time, King John had brought up the rear guard. In the small area on the front lines, the Portuguese pushed back the Castilian infantry, killing and wounding thousands of them. The remaining Castilians then began to flee from the battlefield.

Christian kingdoms of Spain. Portugal benefited by support-
ing the monarchy and, as a result, the Portuguese advanced in
culture and prosperity. During the reign of Ferdinand (1367–
1383), the policy of goodwill among the Portuguese came to
an end and the people chose to end the monarchy. In 1383, the
king of Portugal died, leaving a daughter, Beatrice, who was
married to King John I of Castile. The Castilians claimed the
throne, but the Portuguese council of noblemen—who ruled
Portugal along with the king—chose John, Ferdinand's brother,
as the new ruler. In retaliation, John I invaded Portugal, with
the support of many Portuguese nobles who wanted him to be
king. The Castilians laid siege to the city of Lisbon, but their
army was forced to retreat when a terrible plague broke out in
their ranks. A year later, a large Castilian army returned. This
time they were defeated at the battle of Aljubarrota. This victory established the independence of Portugal.

John I (1357–1433)

The victory at Aljubarrota over the Castilians established John
I of Portugal and his family—the House of Asiz—as the rulers
of Portugal. Among the soldiers that had assisted the Portuguese at the battle were several hundred English archers. The
Portuguese had maintained a close diplomatic relationship
with England in the past. A year after the battle, John signed
a "perpetual alliance" with the English, according to historian
David Birmingham. He also married Philippa of Lancaster, the
granddaughter of an English king, Edward III.

King John also launched Portugal on an era of expansion
that would eventually take its explorers to India. In the eighth
century, as Muslim armies had marched across Africa, they
conquered the city of Ceuta. The city is located in Morocco in
northern Africa, across from the southern tip of the Iberian
Peninsula. From Ceuta, the Muslims had an ideal location
for launching their invasion of Spain and Portugal. In later

OANNES QVARTVS TVGALIÆ R

King John I of Portugal, also known as King John the Great, was known to be a kind ruler with a love of knowledge and culture. During his rule, Portugal prospered. The country acquired new territories and wealth, and his conquest of the Muslim port of Ceuta on the North Africa coast in 1415 eventually led to Portuguese exploration around the world.

centuries, Muslim pirates from Ceuta raided European shipping in the Mediterranean.

Ceuta and Morocco acted as a lure to the Portuguese for several reasons. The Portuguese, who had driven out the Muslims from their kingdom, now wanted to take the crusade into North Africa. They hoped to drive back Islam and spread the teachings of Christianity. According to historian David Birmingham, the nobles of Portugal were also interested in acquiring more land that would become available to them with the conquest of Ceuta.

Finally, Ceuta was an important commercial center. Wheat grown in the area was shipped to other parts of North Africa as well as to western Europe. In return, silver from Europe was shipped by Italian merchants to Ceuta to trade for far more valuable gold. As Birmingham wrote, "much of the Mediterranean world's gold came from West Africa via the Moroccan camel caravans," taking the gold across the Sahara Desert to the coast. "Portuguese merchants therefore aspired to capture the desert markets of the northern Sahara and to dominate the European supply of foreign gold." Many nations had begun using gold coins in this period, so gold was in great demand throughout Europe.

In 1415, the Portuguese mounted an invasion of Ceuta, aimed at driving out the Muslims and taking control of the city. John hoped that the fall of Ceuta would enable the Portuguese to extend their rule along the North African coast. Participating in the expedition against Ceuta was one of John's sons, Henry. His experience there helped propel him into a career that laid the foundations for a new Portuguese empire.

Portugal in the Fifteenth Century

Ceuta seemed a likely choice for a quick strike by Portuguese military forces. It lay at the western end of the Mediterranean Sea, guarding its entrance and protecting the Muslim territories along the coast. The city was located near the end of a long peninsula that jutted out into the Mediterranean. At its tip was a huge hill, over 600 feet high, known as Monte Almina. The Muslims had built stout defenses into the hillside, and an invading army would be forced to capture them to take control of Ceuta and the rest of the peninsula.

As it traveled from Lisbon into the Mediterranean, the Portuguese expedition was forced to battle unfavorable winds. The troops were also struck by plague, which had started in Lisbon and probably caused the death of King John's wife, Queen Philippa, before the troops left on the campaign. When they finally reached Ceuta, a storm drove King John and his ships out of the harbor and across the Mediterranean to Iberia. At this point, some of the king's advisers urged him to give up the

PRINCE HENRY
OF
PORTUGALL

HONI·SOIT·QVI·MAL·Y·PENSE

CEUT.

In 1415, Henry the Navigator, along with his brothers and his father, conquered Ceuta. He was determined to locate the source of the West African gold trade, find the Christian kingdom of Prester John, and stop the pirate attacks on the Portuguese coast. He later sponsored voyages that brought back numerous African slaves and goods.

expedition and return to Lisbon. Nevertheless, Prince Henry wanted his father to continue the campaign, and the king agreed.

The fleet returned to Ceuta. By this time, the Muslim commander had reduced the size of his garrison, believing that the Portuguese would not return. King John began the attack with an artillery bombardment of the city's defenses, and then his troops—led by Prince Duarte—came ashore and stormed the Muslim defenses on Monte Almina. Henry was also involved in the assault, overcoming the Muslim defenders on the hillside and spearheading the attack toward the city that lay beyond. As Peter Russell wrote in his book *Prince Henry "the Navigator," A Life,* "[W]hen the attackers broke through the gates of the city proper, Henry ran so far ahead of those with him that he found himself on his own and cut off in a side street by the enemy." Fortunately he was seen by "an old friend and mentor [who] lost his own life when rescuing the over-bold glory seeker from the danger into which he had thus put himself. It was at Ceuta that Henry . . . earned himself among his peers his lifelong reputation as an exceptionally brave but also impetuous and imprudent soldier."

The Portuguese victory at Ceuta sent a signal to the rest of Europe that King John's small kingdom was about to become a powerful force on the world stage. The Portuguese themselves believed that they now held the "gateway and key to all Africa," according to Russell. Instead of placing one of his older sons in charge of the city, King John appointed Henry to run Ceuta along with Governor Pedro de Meneses, a veteran soldier. As Russell wrote, Henry was the king's favorite son and John wanted to reward him. Over the next few years, Henry gained valuable experience overseeing the new Portuguese colony. Food supplies had to be sent to the Portuguese garrison in the city, which meant organizing ships to carry them. The Muslim mosques were transformed into Christian churches. This was part of the Portuguese effort to defeat Islam and spread Christianity. Henry and his father, the king, also tried to expand the Christian community in Ceuta, but most Portuguese did not want to leave their homeland to live there. So criminals were released from prison to live and work in Ceuta. Prince Henry also began operating his own ships out of Ceuta, preying on Muslim merchant vessels in the Mediterranean.

Meanwhile, King John had given another honor to his son. He had asked the pope to appoint him head of the Order of Christ. Founded in the early fourteenth century by King Denis of Portugal, the Order of Christ was a religious order of knights. Their main responsibility was to help defend Portugal against the Muslims. The Order was provided with large tracts of fertile farmland to support it and over the next century its members had grown very wealthy. King John decided to take over the Order because the Muslim threat had disappeared and the Order of Christ had refused to participate in the campaign against Ceuta.

When Henry was appointed head of the Order in 1420, he also took control of its wealth. This would help him finance his expeditions along the coast of Africa over the next three decades.

Expeditions in the Atlantic

The successful military campaign against Ceuta helped persuade Henry to consider other expeditions. Off the coast of Africa in the Atlantic Ocean lay the Canary Islands and the islands around Madeira. The Castilians had already established small colonies on the Canary Islands, which were also inhabited by native tribes. The islands were a rich source of resin known as dragon's blood—a red substance taken from the dragon tree—used to dye clothing. Henry disregarded the Castilian claims to the islands, and in 1424 launched an invasion of the islands. This time he did not meet with the same success he had achieved in Ceuta.

The Portuguese were defeated by the local tribesmen and forced to give up their plans to establish a new colony.

Henry then turned his attention to the islands of Madeira, which lie only 370 miles (about 600 kilometers) from Morocco. These islands had no inhabitants, and they had not been colonized by any European nations. However, sailors had visited them, noting the vast forests on the islands, and they had appeared on maps since the fourteenth century. Many Portuguese leaders, however, believed that an expedition to Madeira, like the campaign in the Canaries, was a waste of time. Henry refused to listen to them and began to colonize the islands during the 1420s.

Like the Canaries, Madeira was a valuable source of dragon's blood as well as timber for building ships. The islands also had a good climate for growing wheat, sugarcane, and grapes for making wine. Indeed, Madeira became one of the most popular wines in western Europe. Henry was given control of the islands by the Portuguese king and made money off the sale of its products. Peter Russell wrote that it "also brought him new prestige and political power as a leader who, by once again ignoring the voices of skeptics and following his own hunches, had succeeded in moving the territorial frontier of Portugal into the Ocean Sea."

Portugal had also taken the first steps that would lead its explorers along the coast of Africa.

The African Expeditions

Henry never visited the settlements in Madeira. In fact, he seemed to have very little interest in going to sea. Instead, from his headquarters near Sagres, on the southern coast of Portugal, he planned more expeditions. "At heart, a dreamer, a scholar and a monk, he had the brain of a . . . man of business," according to historian K. G. Jayne, as well as "the initiative and dynamic will which enabled him to [transform] his dreams into facts." His office at his home near Sagres "would be furnished as barely as a convent cell," Jayne continued, "the walls inlaid with painted tiles representing, in all likelihood, scenes of Biblical life, or adventures afloat. One can picture Prince Henry amid such surroundings, wearing . . . monkish garb . . . a stark ascetic figure, with deep-set eyes."

During the 1430s, his mind turned to the islands known as the Azores in the Atlantic Ocean. They are located about 900 miles (1,500 kilometers) west of Portugal. Here Henry began to establish colonies, and the colonists started growing wheat and planting vineyards to produce wine. Prince Henry's main interest ranged southward along the western coast of Africa. For many years, Europeans believed that the farthest south that they could sail along the African coast was Cape Bojador in present-day Western Sahara. There the winds and sea were so strong and the fog so thick that sailors feared to travel any farther. Henry refused to be bound by these fears and sent out his ships to prove that they could sail farther south.

In 1434, his mariners reached Cape Juby, which they mistook for Bojador, and later reached Cape Bojador itself. Henry's explorers found no winds or currents there to prevent them from sailing even farther south. Once again, Henry had proven that he knew more about navigation and exploration than other so-called "experts." While the prince was motivated by what he said was scientific interest, there were other motives driving him onward as well. One of these was proving himself right and increasing his own fame throughout western Europe. He was also driven by the desire to find the location of gold mines in Africa that supplied Muslim traders with the gold that they offered for sale to Europe. If these fell under Portuguese control, Henry and Portugal could grow even richer.

Henry was also driven by the desire to spread Christianity to Africa. He believed that somewhere in central Africa might be a large river or gulf that might enable Portuguese ships sailing down the coast to travel inland and link up with an African Christian king named Prester John.

Over the next few years, Henry kept sending out his sailing vessels, urging them to travel farther and farther southward. These vessels were primarily caravels, usually three-masted sailing crafts with lateen sails. Built from corkwood, they were approximately 65 to 100 feet long (about 35 meters) and about 20 to 25 feet (about 8 meters) wide. They carried cannon for

PRESTER JOHN

For several centuries, Europeans had talked about a great king in Africa, who was known as Prester (Priest) John. Some experts believed that he was a direct descendant of the wise men who had visited the infant Jesus in Bethlehem. During the twelfth century, a letter supposedly written by Prester John had been sent to Emperor Manuel Comnenus, a Christian king, who ruled in Constantinople. According to this letter, Prester John governed a great kingdom, with 72 lesser kings, from his capital in Ethiopia. His army of 100,000 soldiers was poised to recapture the Middle East from the Muslims and return it to Christianity. Europeans believed that Prester John was much richer than any other monarch, with great stores of gold in his kingdom to finance his wars against the Muslims. The possibility that Prester John existed and was waiting to conclude an alliance with Christian kings to fight the Muslims fired the imagination of many princes, including Prince Henry of Portugal. He hoped to discover a great African gulf along the coast, called the Sinus Aethiopicus, which would take his sailors inland to Prester John's kingdom. Together they would drive the Muslims out of Africa.

defense. On each side of the prow was a painted eye, and each of the lateen sails carried the red cross of the Order of Christ. The lateen sails enabled the caravels to take full advantage of the wind and they could move at about six knots—or miles—per hour. The crew of each caravel included a captain, a pilot to navigate the vessel, a scrivener who kept a record of the voyage and its trade, as well as a crew of seamen.

Some of the caravels were very light with no storage space, allowing them to travel inland up shallow rivers. As the sailors traveled, they took soundings along the rivers to ensure that the caravels did not get stuck on a sandbar or strike sharp rocks that might cause a leak. The sounding line had a plummet—or weight at one end—to make it sink into the water. At intervals of every two or three fathoms—a fathom is six feet—the line was marked by leather strings.

In 1435, two of Henry's captains, Gil Eanes and Afonso Gonçalves Baldaia, traveled beyond Bojador. The following year, Portuguese explorers reached the Río de Oro, in Western Sahara. In 1441, they had reached Cape Blanco in present-day Mauritania. Then they sailed south of the cape to Arguin Island. In 1443, Henry persuaded the government of his nephew, King Afonso V, to give him a monopoly over all trade south of Bojador. Portuguese merchants were eager to help Prince Henry finance his expeditions so they could share in this monopoly.

At first the Portuguese assumed that they would find towns along the coast where they could conduct trade. They hoped to barter linen cloth for gold, black slaves, antelope skins, and sweet-smelling musk. Soon they realized that the trade was conducted by Arab merchants who came irregularly to the coast. And they were not interested in Portuguese linen but only in traditional clothing worn among the native people of Africa.

To understand the trading system better, one of Henry's assistants, João Fernandes, offered to travel inland and spend time living among the tribes. In 1444, he spent seven months on his journey of discovery before returning to the coast where he embarked on a Portuguese caravel that was waiting for him. Fernandes reported that horses were in great demand among the people who lived in the interior as well as wheat. He also told Henry that gold was plentiful and available to be traded for the goods that the native people wanted.

Over the next few years, the Portuguese established a permanent trading post at Arguin Island, just south of Cape Blanco. The trading post, called a factory, was fortified with stout walls and became a model for other factories that the Portuguese would establish in India.

Meanwhile, Portuguese explorers continued to push farther south. In order to open up trade in the area, according to Peter Russell, the Portuguese began to use the same pattern. "[T]he Prince's men would land in force to intimidate the local inhabitants and to take one or two prisoners [slaves] so that these could be taken to Portugal to be quizzed for information by the Prince personally, or by one of his advisers. If the local people seemed willing to trade, then no further military action might be taken but usually the Portuguese, treating them as their natural enemies, launched . . . armed assaults."

By 1448, however, the Portuguese had stopped trying to intimidate the local people. According to Russell, they had discovered that the people living along the Senegal River and Cape Verde, which the Portuguese reached by 1444–1447, were much fiercer and could not be intimidated. Their larger armies proved to be more than a match for the much smaller Portuguese forces. So the explorers turned to peaceful bartering and trading.

At Arguin, the merchants from Portugal bartered wheat and other items for gold and slaves. For centuries, Muslim traders had brought black slaves from central Africa to ports along the Mediterranean. Slavery was accepted in western Europe, where slaves served in the households of wealthy Europeans and worked on sugar plantations located on islands such as Crete and Sicily. Men such as Prince Henry thought nothing of purchasing slaves and bringing them to Portugal or selling them to merchants from other nations in Europe. In the past, captured Muslims had become slaves on the Iberian Peninsula. The Portuguese began to introduce black slaves to the peninsula from Africa, whom they had purchased from Muslim merchants.

The first slaves arrived in Portugal in 1444. They were sold at a slave mart in Lisbon. Author Hugh Thomas in his book *The Slave Trade* quoted an observer who said, "What heart could be so hard as not to be pierced with piteous feeling to see that company? For some kept their heads low, and their faces bathed in tears, looking one upon another. Others stood groaning very dolorously, looking up to the height of heaven." As they were sold off, families were separated, and their members were never likely to see each other again. One-fifth of the money received from the sales went to Prince Henry, while the rest was given to any merchants who had helped pay for the slave expedition.

As their trading operations pushed southward toward the Senegal River and Cape Verde, the Portuguese slave trade continued. Often the Portuguese bartered horses for slaves. The profits that were made in the slave trade were very large. For a single horse, the Portuguese could purchase from 25 to 30 slaves. An estimated 800 slaves annually were being shipped back to Portugal by Prince Henry's traders in 1455.

While many of Henry's ships' captains were Portuguese, sailors from other parts of Europe also signed on with the prince's expeditions. Among them was an Italian named Alvise da Cadamosto who led an expedition up the Gambia River in 1455. In this area, which the Portuguese called Guinea, they encountered the Mandinka people who refused to trade with them and were afraid that the Portuguese were cannibals. Attacked by the Mandinka with bows and arrows from their canoes, Cadamosto

In the mid-fifteenth century, Portuguese interest in West African gold deposits shifted to a much more readily available commodity—slaves. For 200 years, from 1440–1640, Portugal had a monopoly on the exportation of slaves from Africa.

fired the artillery from his caravels. At first, the Mandinka retreated but later resumed their attack. As a result, Cadamosto and his men left the Gambia and returned to Portugal.

A year later, Cadamosto returned to Africa and once again headed south to Guinea, hoping to establish a Portuguese foothold along the Gambia River. This time he was given permission to meet with a local ruler, named Batimansa, who realized that the Portuguese were not cannibals. The Portuguese also opened up trade with the Mandinka, primarily for slaves.

Henry continued to send out expeditions as far south as present-day Sierra Leone in Africa until his death in 1460. In directing these voyages, the prince had been driven by a

PAPAL BULLS

The pope in Rome was among the most powerful leaders in western Europe. Many Europeans were Catholics who regarded the pope as the leader of their religion. During the 1450s, the popes issued a series of statements, called Papal Bulls, giving their blessing to the explorations of the Portuguese and Henry the Navigator. In one bull, issued in 1452, the pope authorized the Portuguese to go to war against the Muslims and capture their territory because they were opposed to the teachings of Christianity. A second bull, issued in 1455, by Pope Nicholas V, praised the work of Prince Henry, his efforts to colonize Madeira, and his explorations along the African coast. The pope also singled out Henry's attempts to drive back the Muslims and convert native tribespeople to Christianity. As a result, Pope Nicholas said that the Portuguese had earned a monopoly of trade in all the areas that had been conquered as well as any additional territories that might be occupied in the future south of Cape Bojador and eastward to the Indies. A final bull issued by Pope Calixtus III in 1456 gave the Order of Christ special permission to direct the spiritual and religious lives of all the regions conquered by the Portuguese.

variety of motives. These included a crusading spirit to drive back the Muslims and convert as many people as possible to Christianity. In fact, he justified enslaving African people by saying that he intended to convert them. The search for gold was another motive, although the Portuguese never found the gold mines that lay in the African interior. Although Portugal was successful in establishing trading posts along the coast, they never overcame the resistance of the tribes that lived farther inland. As a result, Portuguese sea captains had to trade with them for gold.

Finally, Henry was also motivated by his own interest in exploration and the fame that he might achieve from his discoveries. Many people had doubted the wisdom of spending money for these voyages. Prince Henry had shown that they could be profitable, especially the slave trade. Nevertheless, the money that Henry had spent on his voyages exceeded what he had earned from them. And at his death, wrote C.R. Boxer in *The Portuguese Seaborne Empire, 1415-1825,* "he died deeply indebted." Still, Henry had laid the foundation for additional voyages that would take the Portuguese to the tip of Africa and on to India.

Portugal Becomes the Center of Exploration

ABOUT 1469, VASCO DA GAMA WAS BORN AT SINES ON THE southwest coast of Portugal. Sines consisted of little more than a cluster of cottages in a town of folk who fished for their livelihood. His father, Estêvão da Gama, was a Portuguese knight and the governor of Sines. Estêvão received a small revenue from taxes on soap making. Da Gama's mother was Doña Isabel Sodré, a descendant of the household of Prince Diogo, son of King Edward I of Portugal and governor of the military Order of Christ. Estêvão was a member of the Order of Santiago, named after Saint James. James was one of the original disciples of Jesus Christ, and a famous shrine had been erected in his honor at Santiago de Compostela in Spain. Founded about 1170, the Order of Santiago was a military and religious group established to help drive the Muslims out of Portugal.

There are almost no records of da Gama's childhood. He may have studied at Évora, in central Portugal, where he mastered mathematics as well as navigation and later astronomy. All of these subjects prepared him for the role that he would later play in Portugal's age of exploration.

While he was growing up, Vasco may have heard his father talk about the voyages that were sent out to Africa under Afonso and his successor, John (João) II, who became king in 1481. King John believed that it was not sufficient for Portugal to continue sending voyages to Africa or establish a few trading posts. His goal was to take control of these areas by building fortified castles along the coast. In 1481, King John sent one of his navigators—Diogo d'Azambuja—south to establish a fort called St. George of the Mine along the Gold Coast. Later known as Elmina, it was designed to enable the Portuguese to monopolize the gold trade with the interior of Africa. At Elmina, according to historian C.R. Boxer, the Portuguese bartered for gold and slaves with a variety of trade goods. These included wheat that was grown at their colony in Morocco, cloth from places like England and France, and glass beads from Germany.

Accompanying Azambuja were two mariners named Christopher Columbus and Bartolomeu Dias. Columbus, an Italian, had traveled to Lisbon in the 1470s to visit his brother who lived there. As a result of the expeditions led by Prince Henry and the mariners who came after him, Lisbon had become the center of overseas exploration. Mariners from many parts of Europe had come to live in Lisbon where they hoped to persuade the Portuguese king to let them lead a new expedition. Columbus was fascinated by India, the islands of the Far East, and, especially, China. He carefully read the reports compiled by Marco Polo—a thirteenth-century adventurer who had visited the Chinese court.

Like other mariners who lived in Lisbon, Columbus believed that China might be reached by sailing westward across the Atlantic Ocean. Indeed, some experts thought that there might be a great northwest passage through the Arctic Ocean located south of the North Pole that would take mariners on to the Indies. Others disagreed, believing that the best way to reach the Indies might be to sail around the tip of Africa. Columbus even proposed to King John that he lead an expedition westward to reach the Spice Islands of the Far East. The king discussed this idea with his advisers and geographers, who believed that a much better route to India lay around the tip of Africa.

In 1482, King John sent a member of his staff named Diogo Cão on a mission to establish Portuguese claims along the West African coast. On his voyage, Cão carried a supply of stone pillars with crosses on them. He intended to plant one of these at each point where he came ashore, claiming the territory for Christianity and Portugal. In April, his caravels reached a point along the coast where a huge river emptied into the Atlantic Ocean. By talking with the people who lived in the area, Cão learned that they called the river the Zaire—located in present-day Congo. On a nearby cliff, his sailors carved the words "Hither came the ships of the illustrious King Dom John II of Portugal," according to historian K.G. Jayne.

Cão sailed back to Lisbon in 1484, where he prepared for a second voyage southward. This time he returned to the Congo, and planted two more stone pillars along the coast. He traveled as far as Cape Cross and Walvis Bay in present-day Namibia, not far from the tip of Africa. After planting his second pillar at Cape Cross, he returned to Portugal.

Meanwhile King John II was pursuing other explorations. These were aimed at continuing Prince Henry's efforts to link up with Prester John in Ethiopia. In addition, King John hoped to find a route to the Indies so Portugal could participate in the spice trade. In pursuit of this goal, he sent out two men in 1487—Pêro da Covilhã and Afonso de Paiva.

While Covilhã was heading overland toward the Indies, King John II had sent out another expedition on a similar mission down the coast of West Africa. This voyage was under the command of Bartolomeu Dias, a Portuguese aristocrat. He had already gained experience in African exploration during the expedition of Diogo d'Azambuja. Dias's mission included three ships—the *São Cristóvão*, which he commanded, the *São Pantaleão*, under the command of João Infante, and a supply ship. After leaving Portugal in 1487, the expedition reached the Congo and entered Walfish Bay, where he planted a stone column, much like Cão.

Dias's expedition then headed southward, where the ships were blown off course by powerful storms. As a result, the expedition was blown beyond the tip of Africa into the South Atlantic Ocean. After the winds had died down, Dias sailed eastward, hoping to spot land. Seeing none, he steered his ships northward, eventually reaching Mossel Bay, on the tip of Africa. Dias continued sailing eastward along the coast, eventually reaching the Great Fish River. At this point, the coast turns northeast, and Dias realized that he had rounded the southern tip of Africa. This was a major accomplishment for the Portuguese, as now they could direct trade relations with the Far East.

His sailors, by this time, wanted to return to Portugal, so Dias headed home. Passing the southernmost point of Africa, where the seas were rough, he called it Cape Tempestuous. In December 1488, Dias arrived home in Lisbon. After reporting on his voyage to King John, the king decided to rename the southern tip of Africa the Cape of Good Hope.

Portugal and Castile

In his book *The Career and Legend of Vasco Da Gama,* historian Sanjay Subrahmanyam wrote that there was not strong support to continue the voyages around Africa to India. This was "partly because of the [uncertainty] concerning its economic advantages compared to the traditional overland routes." In addition, the Portuguese were fearful that they could not defend the route if they were drawn into an economic rivalry with Castile. This rivalry had already begun during Prince Henry's time when the Portuguese had attacked the Canary Islands, hoping to take control of them from Castile. Then, in 1492, Columbus sailed on his famous voyage to America, financed by King Ferdinand of Castile and Queen Isabella of Aragon. Columbus hoped to establish a spice route to India by sailing westward and he wanted to claim the route for Spain.

Commenting on a trade route to India, sixteenth-century Portuguese historian João de Barros wrote that it

> was a state that was rather remote for it to be conquered and kept [and] it would so weaken the forces in Portugal that it would lack the one necessary for conservation [defense]. Even more so, for once it was discovered, this Kingdom would face new competitors, which had already been experienced in what transpired between the King Dom João and King Dom Fernando of Castile.

Indeed, so concerned were the Portuguese about this rivalry that they signed a treaty with Castile in 1494. Known as the Treaty of Tordesillas, it was based on papal bulls issued by Pope Alexander VI. This treaty divided the world between Portugal and Castile, giving all the land lying 100 leagues west (about 150 miles or 241 kilometers), and later revised to 370 leagues (about 550 miles or 885 kilometers) west of the Azores and Cape Verde, to the Castilians while the lands lying east of the line went to Portugal. Since the Indies lay east of the line, the Portuguese would now begin their voyages to reach it. The prize was control of the spice routes.

The Spice Routes

It is easy to take spices, like pepper and cinnamon, for granted in the twenty-first century because they are so readily

After 50 years of exploration, the Portuguese finally reached Elmina on the Gold Coast of Africa in 1471. The Portuguese built a fort, St. George of the Mine, or Elmina Castle, which became the first trading post built on the Gulf of Guinea and, eventually, one of the most important stops on the Atlantic Slave Trade.

available in supermarkets and relatively inexpensive. But for many centuries, spices were among the world's most prized commodities.

Take pepper, for example. It was grown, almost exclusively, on tall vines along the Malabar Coast in western India. During May and June, powerful monsoon winds blow from the southwest across the Arabian Sea bringing downpours of rain to the Indian coast. The rains nourishes the vines, known as Piper nigrum, producing flowers. Later in the summer, the weather turns hotter and drier. By November, dry monsoon winds begin blowing from the northeast down from the Ghat Mountains. Berries form on the pepper plants, which are harvested in December. Before the pepper berries are completely ripe, they are picked, boiled in water, and dried in the sun. They darken, forming the black peppercorns that are ground into black pepper. The vines also produce white pepper if the berries are harvested later, as well as green peppercorns if they are pickled in saltwater.

Once the peppercorns were harvested, they were gathered up and merchants carried them to markets across the world. Merchant caravans traveled northward to the Hindu Kush Mountains, through the Khyber Pass and into Afghanistan. Then they traveled across Persia and on to Babylon in Mesopotamia, the present-day Middle East. In the ancient world, Babylon was the capital of a great empire and a busy trading center from which traders carried the peppercorns to Greece, Italy, and other parts of the Mediterranean world. In addition to this overland route, ships also carried cargos of pepper from India across the Persian Gulf, and over the treacherous shoals and sandbars of the Red Sea to Egypt. Eventually, they reached Alexandria, on the Mediterranean, where merchant vessels carried the peppercorns to many other ports.

In 2008, a team of archaeologists from the University of California, Los Angeles and the University of Delaware uncovered evidence of the spice trade between India and Egypt. According to a report in the journal *Sahara,* the team, led by Willeke Wendrich and Steven E. Sidebotham, found a large supply of black peppercorns weighing about sixteen pounds. They dated these peppercorns to the first century A.D.

As the pepper traveled from one location to the next, the price of these valuable peppercorns kept rising higher and higher because each merchant made a profit on his leg of the journey along the spice route. Cinnamon traveled along a similar route from Sri Lanka where it was grown. Farther east on the Molucca Islands, part of present-day Indonesia, cloves— another spice—were grown in tall trees. From the Moluccas, they were shipped to India and on to the West.

Spices were highly prized in the ancient world because of their taste. They were used to flavor meat and sauces, which could taste very bland without any seasoning. The Greek physician Hippocrates believed pepper was a powerful medicine. And the Egyptians also used pepper, wrote Jack Turner in his book *Spice: The History of A Temptation,* as a preservative for dead bodies—part of the process of preserving them as mummies.

In the first century B.C., Egypt was conquered by Roman armies under the command of Caesar Augustus. The Roman emperor also took over a series of ports on the Arabian Peninsula, where Arab merchants had grown rich working as middlemen for the spice trade. Once in control of these ports, the Romans now ran the spice trade between India and the Mediterranean world. Each year, an armada of 120 ships sailed down the Red Sea and headed eastward. Almost a century earlier, a Greek sailor named Eudoxus realized that by using the monsoon winds blowing eastward in the spring and westward in the fall, sailing ships could cut the time of the trip to India and back again by half. Eudoxus apparently received this information from an Indian sailor marooned in the Red Sea.

Some of the Roman ships stopped along the coast of East Africa on their way to India. Here men purchased ivory, slaves, wild animals, and ebony. Then the Roman sailors headed east across the Arabian Sea to India. They brought glass, tin, coral, and, above all, gold coins to trade with the Indian merchants for pepper and other spices. Some of these, such as cloves and nutmeg, came from the Molucca Islands. Aided by winter monsoon winds, the Roman ships returned westward, glided up the Red Sea to its end, and then transferred the spices to caravans that carried them across the desert to Alexandria, Egypt.

Pepper was widely used in the Mediterranean world, especially by the upper classes. The price of a pound of pepper was equal to what the average Roman citizen could earn in two days, according to author Jack Turner. Therefore, only the wealthy could afford it. A pound of cinnamon was far more expensive, selling at more than a Roman soldier might earn in an entire year. Nevertheless, Roman aristocrats enjoyed pepper, cinnamon, and other spices on their food. Indeed, they kept pepper in silver pots on their tables. Roman recipes, according to Turner, often included the words "sprinkle on pepper and serve."

Spices in the Medieval World

By the third century A.D., the power of the Roman Empire was in decline. Powerful German tribes were invading from the north and an African tribe had taken over much of the Red Sea area. Trade with India declined, gold coins became scarcer, and the price of pepper skyrocketed. In the fifth century, when the Visigoth leader Alaric brought his armies to the outskirts of Rome, he accepted a large supply of pepper as well as gold and silver as a bribe for not destroying the city. In the eighth century, the Venerable Bede, a Benedictine monk and an English historian, left a handful of pepper to friends upon his death—it was among his most valuable possessions.

During the Middle Ages, spices were a product used only by the wealthy because they were so expensive. It is estimated that 1,000 tons of pepper (*bottom left*) and 1,000 tons of other common spices were imported into western Europe during the late fifteenth century. Whoever controlled the spice trade became rich; therefore Spain and Portugal became rivals for control of the trade routes to the Indies.

Although spices might be scarce, they continued to be traded through Constantinople by merchants of the Byzantine Empire. Founded in the fourth century A.D. by Emperor Constantine, the empire controlled present-day Turkey and large areas of southeastern Europe as well as the current Middle East. Byzantine merchants traveled to India and Sri Lanka to gather spices and shipped them across the Mediterranean as far as Spain.

In the eighth century, however, the spice trade was disrupted by Muslim armies that swept out of the Arabian Peninsula and conquered vast areas from North Africa to India. "Within a century," according to Turner, "the great Islamic merchants had established themselves along the spice routes of both land and sea, from Malabar in India to as far west as Morocco. By camel and dhow (a type of sailing ship), traders and mariners fanned out east even to China and the Moluccas . . . .Where there were spices there were Muslims."

The Muslims continued to use Alexandria as a seaport to distribute spices to the rest of the Mediterranean world. They traded with merchants in Constantinople, as well as Italian traders. Pavia in northern Italy, for example, became a center of the spice trade, along with other Italian cities like Venice. Their merchants traded directly with the Muslims, although trade with them was technically forbidden by the Catholic Church. Although spices in Europe were nowhere near as plentiful as they had been in the ancient world, well-to-do people continued to use them. Indeed, it became a symbol of wealth. Since gold coins were scarce, peppercorn and other spices even became a substitute for money.

During the eleventh century, Pope Urban II launched a crusade from western Europe to retake Jerusalem and the Holy Lands, which had fallen under Muslim control. Jerusalem was sacred to three great religions—the Jews had made it their capital in the ancient world; Jesus Christ had died in Jerusalem and, according to Christian belief, risen from the dead; and Muhammad had also risen into heaven from the city.

The European knights succeeded in capturing Jerusalem and reestablishing the Christian religion. They also became exposed to the rich lifestyle of the Muslims in the area who enjoyed the luxuries of sumptuous clothing and fine food seasoned with lots of spices. After the knights returned home, their experience in the Holy Land led to an increased demand for spices in western Europe. This demand was met by the Italian traders, whose ships traveled to Constantinople and Alexandria to bring spices into Europe. The profit in spices reached as high as 1,000 percent, according to Turner, and made some Italian merchants extremely rich.

Again, spices, especially pepper, were in great demand for a variety of reasons. Since the medieval world had no refrigerators, people needed to use other methods to preserve meat. Each fall, livestock was routinely slaughtered so that they would not need to be fed throughout the long European winters. What meat was not immediately eaten was preserved in salt; however salted meat was tough and not very tasty after it was cooked. A spice such as pepper greatly improved the taste. It might also cover the taste of old meat that had gone bad or become slightly rancid. Pepper as well as other spices was also used for fish. Referring to ginger, Portuguese botanist Garcia d'Orta said, "On our days of fish it gives us flavor." The Catholic Church required Europeans to abstain from meat and eat fish on certain days of the year.

Like the ancient Romans, medieval people also used spices in a variety of sauces to add some zest to their meals. Spices were also used to improve the taste of desserts, wine, and ale. Cloves and nutmeg, for example, were served with fruit as a popular dessert. Hot spices were also sweetened and served after a meal to help diners digest their food.

Portugal, Spain, and the Spice Trade

One of the major reasons that Prince Henry had launched his explorations was to gain control of the spice trade from the Muslims and the Italians who had dominated it for centuries.

THE SPICER

In aristocratic families, one of the most important members of the staff was the spicer. His role was to acquire appropriate spices to serve with each meal. In addition, he functioned almost as an in-house pharmacist, mixing together the spices that might be served on silver platters after a meal to help digest the food. Meals among the wealthy were very large with numerous courses, washed down with many bottles of wine and glasses of ale. According to Jack Turner, "The household of King Edward IV [an English king] had an 'Office of Greate Spycerye' [Office of Great Spicery], charged with delivering sugar and spice to the 'Office of Confectionarye' [Office of Great Confectionary] for the preparation of highly sweetened after-dinner spices." Before Henry the Navigator set sail for Ceuta in 1414, he had a lavish meal that included a variety of spices at the end to aid his digestion.

Europe had a heavy demand for these luxuries and enough wealthy people to make the trade very profitable. Spain also wanted to dominate the trade. Indeed, this was one of the major reasons that Ferdinand and Isabella agreed to finance Christopher Columbus's voyage westward. They hoped that Columbus would reach India and open up a direct spice trade that would eliminate the Muslim and the Italian merchants.

As Columbus reached the New World on his first voyage in 1492, according to Jack Turner, he said that he "believed that there were great riches and precious spices in them." Yet, as Columbus searched for these spices, he could not find them. The plants did not seem to be those that grew pepper and other spices. "I do not recognize them," Columbus said, "and this causes me much sorrow." Álvarez Chanca, a physician who accompanied the expedition, said, "There are trees which, I think, bear nutmegs, but they were so far without fruit, and I say that I think this because the taste and the smell of the bark is like nutmegs. . . . There is also found a kind of cinnamon; it is true that it is not so fine as that which is known at home."

The explorers also asked the American Indians whom they encountered whether there were any spices growing in the area. They brought samples of cinnamon and pepper and showed these to the American Indians, but they always responded that the spices were somewhere else. "The Spaniards showed them the cinnamon and pepper and other spices," said Chanca, "that the Admiral had given them; and the Indians told them by signs that there was a lot of it near there to the southeast, but that right there they did not know if there was any."

Cinnamon and pepper did not grow in the New World. The closest that Columbus and his sailors ever came was the discovery that chili peppers grew in the areas where they had landed.

The real spice routes could best be reached by traveling east—not through the Mediterranean and the Red Sea where Muslim and Italian ships dominated the waves—but by going around Africa just as Vasco da Gama had later done when sailing to India.

Da Gama and the Portuguese in India

Since the early fifteenth century, Venice controlled much of the trade routes between Europe and Asia. Prince Henry hoped to use Bartolomeu Dias's route to break the domination Venice held on trade in the region. Dias's return after rounding the Cape of Good Hope confirmed that India was reachable by sea from the east. Pêro da Covilhã and Afonso de Paiva confirmed Dias's findings. With the support of King Manuel I, da Gama aimed to be the one to prove the link between the findings of Dias and those of da Covilhã and de Paiva.

On July 8, 1497, da Gama left Lisbon with a crew of 170 men and a fleet of four ships: the *São Gabriel* (commanded by da Gama), the *São Rafael* (commanded by da Gama's brother Paulo), a caravel named the *Berrio* (commanded by Nicolau Coelho, renamed the *São Miguel*), and a storage ship of an unknown name (commanded by Gonçalo Nunes).

The expedition followed the route taken by the earlier explorers along the coast of Africa via the Cape Verde Islands. On November 4, 1497, they successfully landed on the African coast. For nearly four months, the crew had sailed over 6,000 miles, the longest journey made out of sight of land at that time.

By December 16, da Gama passed the point where Dias had turned back and sailed into territory previously unknown to Europeans. His men wanted to go home and he narrowly escaped a mutiny. In January 1498, the fleet came into Muslim-controlled waters off the coast of Mozambique in East Africa, where he hired a guide from Malindi named Ahmad ibn Majid to help them get the rest of the way to India.

On May 21, 1498, after a voyage of over 10 months, da Gama's ships arrived at Calicut in India. The city was located along the Malabar Coast. As the Portuguese sailed toward the harbor, they saw the Ghat Mountains in the distance. The mountains separated Malabar from the rest of India. Aboard ship, da Gama had included a few released convicts to fill out his crew. One of these men, named João Nunes who understood Arabic, was ordered to go ashore. Typically, when they arrived in a new place, the Portuguese selected a lowly member of the crew, or *degredado*—often a convict—as the first person who made contact with the local population. If the people were not friendly and attacked or killed the degredado, the Portuguese felt that his death would be less of a loss than one of the regular crew members. The crew also knew that they would need to defend themselves if they planned to leave their ship.

After Nunes put ashore in Calicut, he was met by several people who took him to the house of local merchants. "What the devil brought you here?" they asked, according to historian Jack Turner. "We came in search of Christians and spices," Nunes told them. Indeed, da Gama and the Portuguese had undertaken this journey of exploration for both spiritual and material reasons. Nunes was given a small meal of bread and honey by the Muslims and one of them returned with him to the Portuguese ship.

After meeting the sailors who had traveled so far to reach India, the merchant told them, "A lucky venture, a lucky venture! Plenty of rubies, plenty of emeralds! You should thank God for having brought you to so rich a country," according to historian K.G. Jayne.

Calicut was, indeed, a wealthy city, enriched by taxing the trade that came through its port. Muslim merchants from India carried on a lucrative business between Calicut and the Maluccas in present-day Indonesia. They traded cotton cloth from India for spices such as cinnamon. Arabs from the Arabian Peninsula traveled to Calicut, carrying woolen clothing from Europe as well as gold. They traded these items for cotton, a purple dye called indigo, and spices, and brought them back up the Red Sea to Egypt before shipping them to Europe. In addition, some Italian merchants from Venice and other cities participated in the trade between India and the Mediterranean.

The rulers of Calicut as well as other port cities, like Cochin and Cannanur, enjoyed a lavish lifestyle based on their income from the trade. According to historian M.N. Pearson, who wrote *The Portuguese in India,* tax money flowed into the government. "Customs duties [taxes on imported items] and port charges are most obvious here, but we must also include land revenue on areas producing pepper, various taxes and charges to do with its transport and weighing . . . and charges deriving from the role of their ports as entrepots [for shipping items to the Red Sea]."

The ruler of Calicut was a Hindu prince known as a zamorin. The Hindu religion had sprung up in India about 3,000 years earlier. Hindus believe in karma, that is, after their death they would be reincarnated into another life. They carefully follow the principles contained in sacred scriptures, called the Veda. In addition, Hindus live according to a time-honored caste system, with Brahmans—priests and highly educated men—as the highest class and Untouchables at the bottom of the class system.

In southern India, where Calicut was located, Hindu princes were constantly in conflict with each other over control of trade and territory. In other parts of the south, as well as in northern India, Muslim kingdoms vied with each other for power and influence. Both Hindu and Muslim rulers tolerated a variety of religious beliefs. In Calicut, for example, there were Muslim mosques as well as Hindu temples. The zamorin was also content to allow Muslim merchants to dominate the spice trade, as long as he could tax it to support his lifestyle.

> One observer named Abd ur-Razzak described Calicut this way during the 1440s: Security and justice are so firmly established in this city that the most wealthy merchants bring thither from maritime countries considerable cargoes, which they unload, and unhesitatingly send to the markets and bazaars, without thinking in the meantime of any necessity of checking the accounts or keeping watch over the goods.

Da Gama and the Zamorin

Late in May 1498, da Gama was summoned to the palace of the zamorin for a meeting. Accompanied by 13 of his men, he left his ships and traveled into Calicut. It was an exotic land—quite different from Portugal—with tropical rain forests and a variety of unusual wildlife, including leopards, tigers, and elephants. As da Gama and his men traveled through the city, they passed the wooden homes of the local people with their thatched roofs. They also stopped at a large Hindu temple. Inside was a statue that the Portuguese believed was the Virgin Mary, mother of

On May 18, 1498, da Gama met with the zamorin (ruler) of Calicut, India. Da Gama hoped the zamorin would agree to an exclusive trade deal, in which the Arab dealers would be expelled from the region and the Indians would only trade with the Portuguese. Da Gama, however, did not have anything worthwhile to trade, and da Gama and the ruler soon turned against each other.

Jesus Christ. They were convinced that Christendom had already come to India. And they cried "Maria, Maria!" They also saw what they thought were "many other saints . . . painted on the walls, wearing crowns," according to the record kept by the Portuguese on their voyage. "They were painted variously with teeth protruding an inch from the mouth and four or five arms." The Portuguese did not realize that these were Hindu gods, not pictures of Christian saints.

Once they reached the opulent palace, da Gama and his men were brought into a spacious room where the zamorin lay "on a green velvet couch under a gilt canopy, and holding a massive golden spittoon in his left hand, while a cupbearer served him with betel (nuts) from a golden bowl," according to K.G. Jayne. The prince welcomed the Portuguese and encouraged them to trade with local merchants for spices. When the zamorin saw the trade goods that da Gama had brought, he was astounded. They included small items like coral necklaces and woolen shirts. The zamorin expected gold, and he was amazed that the Portuguese expected to trade for spices without this precious item.

After returning to his ships, da Gama and his men brought some of their trade goods onshore, but the Muslim merchants had no interest in them. Nevertheless, da Gama was successful in convincing the zamorin to trade a small amount of pepper for some of the Portuguese goods so the pepper could be taken back to show King Manuel. Then da Gama prepared to leave Calicut for the return voyage.

Before he could leave, however, the zamorin's officials informed him that the Portuguese were expected to pay a large customs duty for the trade goods that they had brought into the city. When da Gama refused, his crew members who were guarding the items onshore were arrested. In return, da Gama locked up some Hindus who had come out to his ships. Eventually, this standoff was resolved when both sides agreed to release their prisoners. Da Gama sailed out of the harbor of Calicut in late August.

The Trip Home to Portugal

Unfortunately, the Portuguese had not waited for an end to the monsoon season, and they encountered heavy winds and storms on their trip southward from India. Many of the crew, including da Gama's brother Paulo, became sick with scurvy. The symptoms of this disease—caused by a lack of vitamin C—include loose teeth and bleeding. Scurvy often leads to death. Approximately 30 members of the crew died during the three-month return voyage from India to Africa. There were not enough crew members to sail the three ships, so they left behind the *São Rafael*, near Mozambique. By July 1499, the fleet finally reached the Azores, a Portuguese archipelago in the Atlantic. Paulo died here a day after their landing. It was probably September before they reached Lisbon where they were welcomed home by King Manuel after a voyage of over two years and only 60 members remaining from da Gama's crew.

Nevertheless, da Gama had proven that a sea route from Portugal to India was possible. It also had the potential of opening up an extremely lucrative trade in spices. In a single bold voyage, the Portuguese found themselves on the brink of taking control of a trade that had been dominated by the Italians and the Muslims for centuries. Indeed, King Manuel began calling himself "King, by the Grace of God, of Portugal and of the Algarves, [the southern provinces of Portugal] both on this side of the sea and beyond it in Africa, Lord of Guinea and of the Conquest, Navigation, and Commerce of Ethiopia, Arabia, Persia, and India."

The Voyage of Cabral

No sooner had da Gama returned to Portugal than King Manuel began planning another voyage. This time he selected Pedro Álvares Cabral to lead a squadron of 13 ships armed with artillery to sail to India and try to take over the spice trade from the Muslim merchants.

Born about 1460, Pedro Cabral was the son of a high-ranking Portuguese government official named Fernao Cabral. Although little of his early life is known, he was probably an experienced navigator or King Manuel would not have chosen him to lead such an important voyage to India. His expedition numbered 1,200 men including Bartholemeu Dias and Nicolao Coelho, two veteran seamen. Leaving Lisbon in March 1500, Cabral headed south and then westward. His ships reached present-day Brazil in April. He claimed the territory for Portugal because it seemed to lie east of the

With directions given to him by da Gama and the support of King Manuel, Pedro Álvares Cabral set out with a fleet of 13 ships to the Indies. He was to establish permanent trade agreements and introduce Christianity wherever he went, even by force if necessary. During the voyage, he became the first European to land on Brazil (*above*), establish a factory at Calicut, and succeed in making many advantageous treaties. Cabral returned from his expedition with 4 out of the 13 ships he started with.

line separating Spanish and Portuguese territories that had been established by the Treaty of Tordesillas. Beginning an eastward voyage in May, Cabral's ships ran into treacherous storms near the Cape of Good Hope. Here Dias's ship sank and he drowned. By July Cabral had reached Mozambique. He then sailed into Malindi in early August, and finally sailed into Calicut in September.

After losing half his ships during a six-month journey, Cabral put into Calicut on September 13, 1500. At first, Cabral was more successful than da Gama had been during the earlier voyage. He reached an agreement with the zamorin to set up a warehouse, or factory, onshore. But the Muslim traders resented the presence of the Portuguese, whom they realized were trying to take over the spice trade.

The Muslims maintained a peaceful trade in the Arabian Sea. Muslim merchants from different areas of the spice routes dominated the trade in specific areas. "Gujuratis," according to historian M.N. Person, "were important in western Indian coastal trade, and participated on other routes also. Middle East Muslims dominated the Calicut-Red Sea Route. In every case, however, this position was achieved by superiority in peaceful commercial competition. We have no evidence of any use of force at all."

The Muslim trading ships were unarmed. By contrast, the Portuguese had arrived with ships that bristled with cannon. As a result, they could easily overpower their Muslim competitors. "Right from the start," wrote M.N. Pearson, "the method was to be force," to take over the spice trade.

At first, Cabral ordered the zamorin to expel all Muslim traders from Calicut. When the zamorin refused, Cabral's sailors demonstrated their power by taking over a Muslim spice ship that was enroute from Calicut to the Red Sea. In response, a riot broke out onshore, and Muslims attacked the Portuguese factory, killing over 50 of the seamen who guarded it. Cabral struck back, unleashing his cannon against Calicut, destroying many of its buildings and driving the zamorin out of his palace. According to Jack Turner, Cabral then "seized or sank all Muslim shipping they could lay their hands on; Muslim merchants were hung from the rigging and burned alive in view of their families ashore."

The Portuguese left the city and traveled to Cochin where the local ruler—having probably learned about what had happened in Calicut—permitted Cabral to set up another factory. The ruler of Cochin also wanted to take advantage of the sour relations between Cabral and Calicut to establish a trading agreement with the Portuguese. Meanwhile Cabral also succeeded in collecting a large supply of spices in Cananor. With all of these spices loaded onto his ship by early 1501, he left the Malabar Coast and began his return voyage to Portugal, arriving there in July.

Cabral's voyage was followed by a smaller expedition comprised of four ships under the command of João da Nova that left Portugal in March 1501 and arrived in Cananor in November. Like Cabral, da Nova also attacked Muslim merchant ships, captured their cargo, and then sank them. Meanwhile the zamorin of Calicut assembled a fleet to attack the Portuguese. But the Muslim ships were driven off near Calicut by da Nova's artillery. The Portuguese then sailed to Cananor where they received permission to set up a factory. Leaving the port in February, they arrived in Lisbon in September 1502.

These expeditions marked the beginnings of Portuguese efforts to establish an empire in the Far East. Vasco da Gama would now play a key role in its success.

Da Gama Returns to India

AFTER RETURNING FROM HIS VOYAGE TO INDIA, DA GAMA HAD received numerous honors from King Manuel. The king had provided him with a generous annual income and named da Gama Admiral of the Indies. He had also been given the noble title *Dom* and was thereafter known as Dom Vasco. About 1501, Dom Vasco married another member of the nobility, Doña Catarina de Ataíde. She was the daughter of Álvaro de Ataíde—mayor of Vila de Alvor—and Maria da Silva, a close friend of King John II.

Following the voyages of da Gama, Cabral, and da Nova, King Manuel was considering another expedition that might take control of the Indian spice trade from the Muslims and the Venetians who had dominated it for so many years. In his biography *The Career and Legend of Vasco da Gama*, Sanjay Subrahmanyam wrote that Venice was worried that the people of western Europe would buy spices directly from the Portuguese instead of paying the high prices demanded by the Venetians.

King Manuel (nicknamed "the Fortunate") supported Portuguese explorers and the development of Portuguese commerce. During his reign, Portugal forged diplomatic alliances and treaties with China and the Persian Empire, and Portuguese explorers, including da Gama and Cabral, were very successful due to his support.

According to fifteenth-century author Girolamo Priuli, quoted by Subrahmanyam, the Venetian merchants would be "like a baby without its milk and nourishment."

Some of King Manuel's advisers were unsure that another expedition made financial sense. Cabral's expedition had been very expensive, and he had returned with only a small load of spices. Meanwhile, he had managed to irritate many of the Indian rulers. Nevertheless, King Manuel decided to send Cabral on another expedition to India. Then he changed his mind.

One reason may have been that Cabral's lack of success finally persuaded the king to appoint someone else. Cabral had also been unable to get along with a powerful sea captain who had accompanied his first expedition. Vincente Sodré had been given an independent command in the expedition and ordered to "guard the mouth of the Strait of the Red Sea," preventing Muslim merchants from entering or leaving the area. Sodré apparently had influence at court, and even more importantly, he was Dom Vasco's great-uncle. At this point, da Gama may have asked that Cabral be replaced as the leader of another voyage to India. In any event, King Manuel decided that Dom Vasco should take command of the expedition, not Cabral.

Da Gama immediately appointed Sodré to a command along with his brother Brás Sodré. The Portuguese assembled 15 well-armed ships for the expedition. In addition, Dom Vasco's first cousin Estêvão da Gama (who had the same name as Dom Vasco's father) was put in charge of five more vessels that would leave Lisbon two months after Dom Vasco.

On January 30, 1502, Dom Vasco and his captains attended Catholic Mass at the Cathedral Church in Lisbon. An observer at the ceremony wrote that da Gama

> dressed in a crimson satin cape . . . lined with ermine, with cap and doublet matching the cape, adorned with a gold chain, approached the king attended by the whole court. . . . And then, he turned to the Admiral, with many

words in his praise and in praise of his late predecessors, showing how by his industry . . . he had discovered all this part of India.

Voyage to India

Dom Vasco's ships left Lisbon on February 10, 1502, reaching the Cape Verde Islands by the end of the month and rounding the Cape of Good Hope in May during a heavy storm. In June, the Portuguese reached Sofala on the east coast of Africa, where they purchased gold from the local ruler. Dom Vasco then headed northward to the island of Mozambique, which he had visited on his first voyage. The Portuguese sent messages to the local ruler at Kilwa on Mozambique, Amir Ibrahim. At first there was no response, so Dom Vasco threatened "bombardment if the ruler were unwilling to come to terms," according to Subrahamanyam. These terms included an agreement to sell gold to the Portuguese and to give them an annual payment of 10 pearls. Amir Ibrahim agreed to these terms to avoid having his territory destroyed by the Portuguese guns.

As the Portuguese were leaving Mozambique, Dom Vasco's cousin Estêvão arrived with the rest of the ships. Together they headed for Malindi but storms forced them to continue northward across the Indian Ocean toward Cananor on the west coast of India, which Dom Vasco reached in early September.

The Portuguese mission was to drive the Muslim merchant ships off the sea. They did not intend to compete with the Muslims peacefully. Because they were followers of Islam and not Christianity, the Portuguese regarded the Muslims as nonbelievers. They were considered a threat to Christianity and, therefore, the Portuguese felt justified in using violence to remove them from the seas.

To accomplish this goal, Dom Vasco's ships waited for Muslim vessels that might be traveling from the Red Sea

On February 12, 1502, da Gama set out for his second voyage, with a fleet of 20 ships, to enforce Portuguese interests. The Muslim merchants were not as eager to trade with the Portuguese, having murdered 50 of Cabral's men in Calicut. After raids on several Muslim ports along the East African coast, da Gama captured the *Meri*, a ship containing Muslim passengers on a return journey from Mecca, and set it on fire, killing 400 men, women, and children aboard.

toward India. In late September, one of these ships appeared, and the Portuguese forced it to stop. The ship was carrying about a dozen wealthy merchants headed for Calicut. One of them, who was in charge of the ship, met with Dom Vasco and offered him a generous amount of money if he would allow the vessel to continue its voyage. But da Gama refused and demanded that all the cargo on the ship should be handed over to the Portuguese. At this the merchant said to him, "When I commanded this ship, they did as I commanded; now that you command it, you tell them!"

Dom Vasco's sailors boarded the ship and took money from the merchants. Then da Gama decided to burn the ship along with all the people—men, women, and children—on board. Some of the passengers managed to put out the fire, and they pleaded with the Portuguese not to kill them. According to one observer, they "waved their gold and silver jewelry and precious stone, crying out to the Admiral that they were willing to give him all that for their lives; some of the women picked up their infants and pointed at them," pleading with him to save them. When da Gama refused to listen, men aboard the ship approached one of the Portuguese vessels and attacked it. They were eventually driven off, and, according to an eye witness quoted by Subrahmanyam, "[A]fter all those combats, the Admiral had the said ship burnt with the men who were on it, very cruelly and without any pity." Nevertheless, he did save the lives of about 20 children, who converted to Christianity.

Dom Vasco claimed that he had taken this action in retaliation for the Portuguese who had been killed by the Indians at Calicut during Cabral's expedition. He may have also decided to send a message to the Indian rulers that the Portuguese were not to be ignored in their effort to take over the spice trade.

Dealing with the Indian Rulers

Following this episode, Dom Vasco began to negotiate with the ruler at Cananor to sell spices to the Portuguese. At first, da Gama stayed on board his ship, fearing that the Indian ruler might try to capture him. Finally, the local ruler agreed to meet Dom Vasco on a pier that had been built in the harbor. The pier had one entrance on the sea and another entrance on land. According to Subrahmanyam, "Gama approached it in a caravel with its [deck] covered in green and crimson velvet, accompanied by the most important men on the fleet, and by boats with flags, trumpets, drums and so on. There was music and dancing, but also the firing of guns by way of salutation." Meanwhile, the ruler of Cananor approached from the other entrance to the pier with several hundred armed men.

Having seen the number of these soldiers, Dom Vasco refused to leave his ship and carried on all of the negotiations from there. The Portuguese eventually learned that the cost of spices had greatly increased since Dom Vasco's last voyage. This irritated da Gama who threatened to bombard Cananor unless the prices were lowered. Instead, he finally decided to leave the city and purchase spices somewhere else.

Meanwhile, Dom Vasco had received a message from the zamorin at Calicut offering to sell him spices. The zamorin sent messengers who said that he would forget about what had happened in the past, arguing that the Portuguese sailors lost by Cabral more than equaled the Indian people killed by Dom Vasco on the ship outside Cananor. However, da Gama was not satisfied and demanded that the zamorin expel all of the Muslim merchants from the spice trade. Then he imprisoned the zamorin's messengers. When the zamorin protested, Dom Vasco replied that he was planning to bombard the city.

Soon afterward Portuguese cannon began firing on the waterfront, destroying many houses along the harbor. Meanwhile Dom Vasco had been stopping ships passing through the harbor, capturing their sailors, and hanging them. By early November, da Gama finally ended the bombardment after leveling a large part of the city and sailed southward to Cochin. Once again, he had sent a message to the local rulers that the Portuguese meant business and should not be resisted.

In Cochin, where news had arrived of the Portuguese bombardment of Calicut, da Gama faced a local ruler, Unni Goda Varma, who was not eager to deal with the Portuguese.

Dom Vasco tried to smooth things over by giving him lavish gifts. In Cochin, Dom Vasco finally succeeded in trading with the local merchants for pepper, cloves, and cinnamon—paying for the spices with Portuguese silver, copper, cloth, and wood. Meanwhile the ruler at Cananor had agreed to trade with the Portuguese, and da Gama sent ships commanded by Vincente Sodré to purchase spices there.

While Dom Vasco was in Cochin, a Brahmin ambassador appeared. He had been sent by the ruler of Calicut and wanted the Portuguese to return to resume negotiations. Da Gama sailed for Calicut and, arriving in the harbor, received messengers from the zamorin who said that a load of spices awaited him onshore. All he had to do was to send some of his

VINCENTE SODRÉ AND HIS BROTHER

Upon his return voyage to Portugal, Dom Vasco had left Vincente Sodré behind with five or six ships. His mission was to intercept Muslim merchant vessels and to provide protection for the new Portuguese factories in Cananor and Cochin. Instead of protecting the factories, however, Sodré and his brother Brás spent most of their time trying to capture Muslim trading ships. The Portuguese were very successful, stopping merchant ships heavily laden with spices and other products. But the booty was taken primarily by the Sodrés while the other ship captains were given very little of value. In April, the Portuguese ships were near Oman on the Red Sea when they were caught in a violent storm. Vincente Sodré lost his life but his brother escaped, only to die shortly afterward. Some historians believe that he was murdered by some of his men who were jealous at not receiving more of the captured cargoes.

sailors there to collect it. Fearing a trap, Dom Vasco kept all of his men on the ships. That evening, under the cover of darkness, a flotilla of 70 or 80 small Muslim ships sailed toward the Portuguese caravels in the harbor. They had reached the ships before Dom Vasco's men could fire their cannon and blow the Muslim vessels out of the water.

A bloody battle broke out that lasted until the following morning. Finally, the Portuguese were reinforced by Vincente Sodré's ships that had arrived from Cananor, and the Muslim attack was defeated. After the battle, Dom Vasco "hanged the envoys whom he still held on the masts of the two caravels, and made it a point to sail up and down the seafront of Calicut with them visible," according to Subrahmanyam.

The Portuguese then returned to Cananor and Cochin to gather loads of spices. Dom Vasco also negotiated an agreement with Unni Goda Varma in Cochin to establish a Portuguese factory there. Da Gama was now preparing to return to Portugal. But before he could depart, the Portuguese were attacked once more by a fleet from Calicut. Once again, Dom Vasco successfully withstood the attack and defeated the zamorin's ships. Meanwhile, many of the merchants from Calicut had decided to leave for Cananor, realizing that the Portuguese could not be defeated and that it made far more sense to trade with them.

In February 1503, Dom Vasco left India on his return voyage to Portugal. Reaching the Cape of Good Hope by the middle of June, food was in short supply aboard the ships. Nevertheless, the sailors finally reached Lisbon in October. They brought with them a large supply of pepper and other spices, including cinnamon. Some of these spices belonged to Dom Vasco, who had carried on his own private trading business. According to one report, he had aboard his own ship silver cups "which served for his own use in the ship as captain," and used these to purchase pepper, ginger, cinnamon, cloves, and nutmeg. As Sanjay Subrahmanyam put it, "Gama thus accumulated not only fame on these voyages, but quite literally a fortune."

The Portuguese Empire in the East

AFTER RETURNING FROM HIS SECOND TRIP TO INDIA, DA GAMA settled down for the next two decades in Portugal. Dom Vasco and his wife, Doña Catherina, had seven children. They had one daughter, Isabella, and six sons: Francisco, the eldest; Estêvão, who later became governor of India; Paulo; Christovão; Pedro; and Alvaro. Paulo, Pedro, and Alvaro all served in Malacca (in present-day Malaysia) during the 1530s and 1540s.

Due to his pension from the Portuguese government, his landholdings, and the money he had made in the spice trade, Dom Vasco was among the wealthiest men in Portugal. Meanwhile, he continued to provide counsel to King Manuel regarding overseas voyages to the Far East. However, the king did not appoint him to lead another expedition back to India. Historian Sanjay Subrahmanyam wrote that King Manuel may have been irritated at Dom Vasco because his uncles, Vincente and Brás Sodré, were trying to get rich in the spice trade rather than guarding Portuguese factories in India. Dom Vasco may

Da Gama brought massive wealth back to Portugal during his voyages. From his second voyage, it is estimated that the value of his loot amounted to about one million dollars in gold. Due to such commanders as da Gama, King Manuel (*seated, greeting da Gama after his return from the Indies*) made Portugal the leading commercial nation of the West.

have even known what they had planned to do but said nothing about it.

What's more, da Gama had traded for spices while in India, which went against the policy of the king. Manuel believed that the government should have absolute control of the trade. As historian M.N. Pearson wrote, the profits on a shipload of pepper could be as high as 260 percent. Pearson further explained that during the 1500s the amount of spices brought from the Far East were equal in value to 7,500 tons of silver. Therefore, King Manuel wanted to control the trade.

This meant that spices could only be carried in Portuguese ships. Every trading ship had to purchase a special pass—called a *cartaz*—from the government. Any ship without a cartaz could be stopped by the Portuguese, its crew imprisoned or executed. Even ships with these passes had to pay another tax— called a customs duty—on all of the spices that they collected. In addition, any merchant who wanted to trade in spices had to purchase storage space on a ship for his merchandise.

Dom Vasco, on the other hand, believed that aristocrats, like him, should have the freedom to trade for pepper and other spices on their own. They should also be permitted to capture Muslim ships carrying spices and keep the prizes. This disagreement with government policy may have created a conflict between Dom Vasco and King Manuel.

Expeditions to the East

Although da Gama remained at home in Portugal, King Manuel sent out other expeditions to India to strengthen Portuguese control over the spice trade. In 1504, an expedition of 11 ships commanded by Lopo Soares de Albergaria left Lisbon in April. Captain-Major Lopo Soares was a member of the nobility whose father had served in King Afonso's government. Lopos Soares had been posted to Elmina during the 1490s before being given command of the expedition to India.

His ships arrived in Cananor in September and then headed for Calicut, where the zamorin wanted to talk with the Portuguese. However, Lopo Soares had been given direct instructions not to make an agreement with the zamorin. "If by chance the king of Calicut sends a message to state that he seeks our friendship and wishes to make up for the damage that we have suffered," read his orders, "listen to him, but your response should be as follows: that you have no orders to make an agreement, but rather to do all the harm you can, to him." Although Lopo Soares talked with the zamorin, nothing came of their discussions. The Portuguese then bombarded Calicut and headed for Cochin.

There they gathered a large supply of pepper as well as cinnamon and cloves and sailed westward back to Portugal. The risky position of the Portuguese in India combined with the high value of the spice trade convinced King Manuel that he had to do far more to defend his trading interests.

In 1505, the king created a new position, called the viceroy of India, to run the Portuguese spice trade and strengthen Portuguese defenses against Hindu and Muslim attacks. King Manuel appointed Francisco de Almeida as the first viceroy. Dom Francisco was an aristocrat who had been a close adviser to Manuel's predecessor, King John II. His strategy, as he wrote to the king, was to "avoid the annexation of territory, build no more fortresses than may be absolutely necessary to protect your factories from a sudden raid. We can spare no men from the navy." He added: "As for the fortresses that you order be built, the more fortresses you build, the weaker your power will be, for your entire force rests on the sea, and if we are not powerful there, we will easily lose all the fortresses." Almeida wanted the Portuguese to rely on the superiority of their navy to control the spice trade and drive the Muslim merchants off the seas.

One of the reasons for Dom Almeida's approach was the lack of manpower in Portugal to run an empire in India.

Portugal was a relatively small country with a population of only about one and one half million people. So few men were available to serve aboard the Portuguese ships that Almeida was forced to take inexperienced sailors and try to train them. These men did not know port (right) from starboard (left) aboard ship. As a result, captains had to guide the sailors who were steering the ship from the helm with onion and garlic. Onion was tied on one side, and the helmsman was told, "Onion your helm!" On the other side was garlic, and the helmsman was ordered to "Garlic your helm!"

Leaving Portugal with about 20 ships and 1,500 soldiers, the expedition stopped at Sofala, Mozambique, and Mombassa. Dom Almeida captured Mombassa after a bloody attack and later captured the island of Zanzibar. These victories helped to solidify Portuguese power in East Africa and drive out Muslim traders.

After arriving in India, Dom Almeida went to work improving the Portuguese defenses at Cochin. Meanwhile he was forced to drive back a naval squadron sent against the Portuguese by the zamorin of Calicut. With so few soldiers and sailors available, Dom Almeida also tried to make an alliance with the Hindu Vijauanagar Empire in southern India. The empire's ruler was considered an enemy by the Muslims as well as by the zamorin of Calicut.

Nevertheless, Almeida still faced powerful Muslim naval forces in the Arabian Sea off the west coast of India. Egypt was governed by Muslim rulers known as the Mamluks. To the east, present-day Turkey and the Arabian Peninsula were controlled by the Ottoman Turks. In 1508, the Mamluks, under the command of Mir Hussain, sent a large fleet of warships eastward to India, heavily armed with artillery. Near the Indian port of Chaul, it defeated a smaller Portuguese naval force commanded by Dom Almeida's only son, D. Lourenço de Almeida, who died during the battle.

The viceroy was so upset at the loss of his son that he gathered together a fleet to avenge his death. A fierce battle broke out between Mir Hussain's navy and the Portuguese ships in February 1509 near the port of Diu in Gujarat. As the battle began, the Muslim and Portuguese vessels traded fire from their heavy guns. Then Dom Almeida's ships sailed toward the enemy, with bowmen from Malabar firing arrows toward the enemy sailors. As the ships drew close together, the Portuguese sailors, using grappling hooks on long ropes, lashed their vessels to those of Mir Hussain's. A bloody struggle then took place aboard the ships, fought with battle axes and long pikes. The Portuguese gradually began to wear down the Egyptians, and their remaining ships eventually retreated.

Dom Almeida had won an important victory that helped to solidify Portuguese control in India. Meanwhile, he had been replaced by another governor, Alfonso de Albuquerque. At first, Dom Almeida did not want to give up his position, but eventually he agreed to return to Portugal. His ships left India in December 1509, reaching Table Bay near the tip of Africa in February 1510. They went ashore for water and began to trade with local tribesmen. The Portuguese stole some cattle, a disagreement occurred, and they were attacked by the tribesmen. During the conflict, Almeida and many of his men were killed.

Albuquerque Establishes an Empire

Dom Afonso de Albuquerque was born outside Lisbon in 1453. He later fought against the Muslims in North Africa during the reign of King Afonso V and became an adviser to King John II. In 1506, he had sailed to India and later captured Hormuz at the mouth of the Red Sea. When Dom Afonso tried to build a fort there to control the trade, his men had refused to support him and he was forced to retreat.

When he became governor, Dom Afonso was fifty-six years old. A small man with a long beard and a large nose, he

AFOMCODAL BVQERQVEGOVE RNADOR

Afonso de Albuquerque was a major figure in the establishment of the Portuguese empire in the East. With the capture of Malacca in 1511, Albuquerque was able to control trade from the East Indies and the coast of China. He later secured the rights to principal strategic points from the east coast of Africa to Malacca, excluding the Red Sea. His policies made Portugal the dominant commercial force in the East until the seventeenth century.

was known as a man of simple tastes. He fought alongside his men, ate with them, and joined them in building fortifications. He was also a stickler for detail, spending long hours pouring over reports about military defenses, the spice trade, and the activities of the Muslims. Dom Afonso believed that he was in a brutal struggle with the Ottoman Turks. "The Turks are powerful," he wrote, "they have much artillery, and know how to build ships like our own. They hate us, and long to destroy all we possess."

Unlike Dom Almeida, Albuquerque believed that the Portuguese had to occupy more territory to solidify their hold on the trading routes to India and farther east. He believed that several strategic points held the keys to these routes. They included Hormuz; Aden, at the mouth of the Persian Gulf; Goa, an important port city lying north of Cochin; and Malacca in present-day Malaysia.

Before undertaking this plan, however, Albuquerque first led an attack on Calicut in early 1510. This was aimed at eliminating a constant thorn in the side of the Portuguese traders. In a fiercely fought battle in which Dom Afonso almost lost his life, the city was captured and the zamorin driven out of his palace.

Albuquerque then turned his attention northward to Goa, one of the busiest ports in western India. It could also become an important base for the Portuguese. As Dom Afonso wrote the king, "In Goa, beef, fish, bread and vegetables are plentiful . . . in Goa there are gunsmiths, armorers, carpenters, shipwrights, everything we require." In a surprise attack, early in 1510, Albuquerque easily conquered the city because its ruler, Yusuf Adil Shah, was away with most of his soldiers.

The Portuguese were unable to hold the city for very long. In May, Adil Shah returned with an overwhelming force of 60,000 soldiers. Although Dom Afonso tried to defend Goa, he was forced to retreat to his ships. Still, before leaving, he massacred most of the residents, including men, women, and children. Having reached the safety of his ships, however, Albuquerque was unable to sail away because of the strong monsoon winds. Gradually his men ran short of food but by that time the winds had finally lessened and the Portuguese were able to leave the harbor.

Albuquerque had not given up his efforts to take control of Goa, realizing how important it was to Portuguese interests in India. In November 1510, he returned with a large flotilla

WAS A MONOPOLY POSSIBLE?

Although the Portuguese hoped to drive out the competition and monopolize the spice trade, this proved to be impossible. As historian M.N. Pearson pointed out, there were many reasons for the Portuguese failure. Although the Portuguese controlled important ports along the coast of India, they had no control over the interior of the country where the pepper was produced. These areas were dominated by powerful local rulers. The harvests were often sold to merchants—paying more than the Portuguese—who took the pepper to the east coast of India, where Portugal had no power.

Some of the pepper was also transported northward to the important trading center of Diu. From here, it was transported by caravans overland into Asia and westward, or it was shipped across the Arabian Sea to Aden. Since Albuquerque had been unsuccessful in capturing Aden, it continued to serve as an important Muslim port. Farther eastward, the Portuguese, according to Pearson, had only about one-third of the trade in cloves and only a small amount of the trade in cinnamon. The rest was carried by other merchants.

(Continues)

(Continued)

Portugal simply lacked enough ships and enough men to have a monopoly of the spice trade. The population of Portugal was small, and the country could not afford to lose many of its own people who were needed to operate farms and fill other jobs. As poet Francisco de Sá de Miranda wrote:

> I have no fear of Castile,
> Whence comes no sound angry of war
> But I'm afraid of Lisbon,
> That at the smell of this cinnamon,
> Unpeoples our kingdom.

The Portuguese also discovered that even maintaining the share that they controlled proved to be very expensive. There was the cost of building the forts and manning them with soldiers. To protect their merchant ships from attack by pirates, the Portuguese had to organize convoys, known as *cafilas*. These were protected by armed ships. The cost of the protection was very high, adding to the expense of maintaining the spice trade. This cut into the profits and made it harder for Portugal to afford to run its empire in the east.

of ships, soldiers, and Hindu allies. In a hard-fought struggle, Dom Afonso's soldiers finally reached the city walls, hoisted their scaling ladders, and drove the Muslim defenders off the battlements, taking control of the city. The Portuguese celebrated their victory with another massacre of Goa's inhabitants before Dom Afonso ordered his men to start rebuilding the city walls so he could maintain control of the port.

Having secured Goa, the Portuguese now looked eastward to Malacca. This was another important port city, which controlled much of the spice trade westward to India and Europe as well as eastward to China. While Europe was a major market for spices, China was an even larger market for pepper grown in Southeast Asia. The Portuguese wanted to control both markets. In April 1511, Albuquerque and his ships headed east for Malacca. This was a wealthy trading city with a large harbor that held merchant ships from many different parts of the world. After reaching the city, Albuquerque sent a message to the sultan demanding that the Portuguese be given land to build a factory there.

When the sultan refused, Dom Afonso prepared to attack the city. Although his troops were greatly outnumbered, they seized a key bridge on an important river outside the city. Meanwhile, Albuquerque had also convinced the local inhabitants—who did not like the Muslim ruler—to stay out of the battle. This removed a large group of soldiers from the city's defenses. From their position on the bridge, the Portuguese slowly drove back the Malaccan defenders. Then, in fierce house-to-house fighting, they succeeded in capturing the city.

Leaving Malacca under the control of some of his men, Albuquerque sailed westward to India. He returned just in time to deal with an attack on Goa by the Muslims. The Muslim army had built a strong fortified position outside the city, manned it with heavy artillery, and from there conducted their siege of Goa. Albuquerque led his ships up to the walls of the fort, and in a hard-fought artillery duel put the Muslim guns out of action. Realizing that the siege was lost, the Muslims retreated from the battlefield.

Then he turned his attention to Aden at the mouth of the Red Sea. In February 1513, with an army of about 2,700 troops and 24 ships, Albuquerque headed toward the Red Sea. Located on a narrow tip of land with strong defenses, the city was very difficult to capture. Still, Dom Afonso believed that the Portuguese must control Aden to safeguard their trade routes. Leading one of the assaulting parties himself, Dom Afonso reached the city's battlements under a hail of fire from its defenders. Yelling "Victory, victory! Portugal! Portugal!" according to historian K.G. Jayne, the soldiers tried to reach the top of the walls on their scaling ladders. Some of the men succeeded in entering the city but they were slaughtered and only one of them, Garcia de Sousa, along with one of his comrades, remained inside in a tower overlooking the walls. When Dom Afonso yelled to him over the noise of battle to retreat, Garcia de Sousa refused. "Save yourself," he said, according to Jayne. "I shall die here." And he was killed.

Eventually, the Portuguese were forced to retreat, without capturing Aden. After returning to India for several months, Albuquerque then decided to launch an attack on Hormuz at the mouth of the Persian Gulf. This was one of the wealthiest ports in the Middle East. As the Muslims in Arabia put it, "The earth is a ring, and Hormuz the jewel set in it." It was the center of a lucrative trade in horses, furs, spices, and many other items.

Hormuz was governed by Rais Ahmad, acting for the king, Turan Shah. As Albuquerque arrived at the city, its rulers agreed to meet with him to discuss Portuguese trade proposals. Although the Portuguese had agreed to enter Hormuz without any arms, they had knives hidden on them. As the meeting with the Muslim leaders began, the Portuguese removed their daggers and attacked Rais Ahmad, who was assassinated. The king was so frightened that he agreed to let the Portuguese take over the city. Nevertheless, they left Turan Shah as head of the government to maintain the allegiance of the people.

Soon afterward, Dom Afonso began construction of a fortress at Hormuz. While the building was under way, he was stricken with a serious illness. Realizing that he might not recover, Albuquerque asked to be taken back to Goa, where he died in December 1515.

Before his death, however, Dom Afonso had laid the foundation of a Portuguese empire in India and the East Indies. He had established new forts, taken control of new territory, and dedicated himself to securing a valuable spice trade that would be controlled by the Portuguese king.

Da Gama and the Portuguese Empire

In 1524, a decade after the death of Albuquerque, Vasco da Gama returned to India. He had been named the new Portuguese viceroy by King João (John) III, who had succeeded to the throne after his father Manuel's death several years earlier. Dom Vasco was 65 years old, and a portrait shows a handsome man with intense eyes and a white beard.

Da Gama had not been to India for more than 20 years. Since that time, the Portuguese had tried to control a lucrative spice trade by conquering strategic points along the trading routes. Under King Manuel, they had spent vast sums of money outfitting fleets and building forts to safeguard this trade. The routes were difficult to defend because they stretched from Malacca in the East, and westward to India, the Persian Gulf, the Red Sea, and the east coast of Africa. Dom Vasco scoffed at the idea of spending so much money on these forts, believing they were a waste of precious Portuguese resources.

Da Gama continued to be richly rewarded in his later years. Already given the title Dom and Admiral of the Seas, he was later named count of Vidigueira and served as an adviser to the king on Indian issues. In 1524, Manuel's successor, John III, appointed da Gama viceroy of India. Da Gama was sent to the subcontinent once more to fix the problems of the incompetent representative there, but he became ill and died in the city of Cochin.

According to the duke of Bragança, a colleague of da Gama's, Dom Vasco

> in my view understood the affairs of India better than anyone else and his vote was that Malacca should be sold . . . and I do not recall whether with Hormuz too a similar bargain should be struck, and that these and all other fortresses in India should be leveled, except Goa and Cochin, it being certain that if in the beginning of the decision to navigate [to India], this had been kept in mind, it would have been wonderful.

King João III agreed with Dom Vasco's policies, which was one of the primary reasons he had been selected to become viceroy of India. Da Gama had also been chosen because he had a reputation as a tough leader who would deal with serious problems that had arisen in the Portuguese empire—namely, waste and corruption. The king had received reports that the Portuguese governors were employing far more officials than they needed. The previous governor, Duarte de Meneses, was also under investigation for using the king's money to carry on his own illegal trade in spices. High-ranking Portuguese officials had also removed the cannon from the forts in India and placed them on their own trading ships to defend these vessels as they conducted illegal spice trading. Meanwhile, other officials were accepting bribes so that local merchants could avoid paying custom duties—taxes that were supposed to be paid on their trading goods.

Sailing for India

Dom Vasco sailed for India with 14 ships in April 1524. Along with him went two of his sons, Estêvão and Paulo, who had received high-ranking positions in the East. Although da Gama was expected to reduce expenditures in India, this did not stop him from traveling there in lavish style. A contemporary historian wrote that he "was served by men bearing silver maces . . . and two pages with gold neck-chains, many . . . body servants, very well clothed and cared for; he also brought rich [bowls] of silver, and rich tapestry . . . and for the table at which he sat brocade cloths."

The expedition rounded the Cape of Good Hope and arrived in Mozambique in August. Before reaching India, three of the vessels were shipwrecked at sea. On a fourth ship, the sailors murdered their captain and decided to become pirates, preying on merchant ships in the Arabian Sea. In September, Dom Vasco finally reached Goa, capital of the Portuguese empire.

No sooner had the new viceroy arrived than he announced a new set of policies designed to save money. Retired soldiers, who had been severely wounded during their service to the empire, were told that they would no longer receive any pensions from the government. Garrisons at forts, such as Chaul, were also reduced, and da Gama intended to reduce the number of employees at the factory in Cochin. The contrast between these policies and Dom Vasco's "viceregal splendor . . . may have been intended to impose Gama's authority and make his presence all the more awe-inspiring," according to historian Sanjay Subrahmanyam, but it created "resentment against a celebrated, powerful and authoritarian viceroy."

Meanwhile, the new viceroy also developed a reputation as a strict disciplinarian with his soldiers. Some of the men who had traveled to Goa aboard Dom Vasco's ships were sick, but he would not permit them to be treated in the local hospital. Da Gama said that "the king, his lord, had no need of hospitals in India, for if they were there, the men would always claim to be sick," according to Subrahmanyam.

While he was in India, Dom Vasco continued sending out ships to stop any Muslim spice traders. Many of them tried to smuggle loads of pepper from the west coast northward to the port of Diu in Gujarat. Nevertheless, the viceroy permitted Portuguese officials to carry on a private trade in pepper. This had been da Gama's policy when he last served in India during the early sixteenth century.

Dom Vasco's return to India, however, turned out to be much shorter than he had expected. Although he had hoped to set a new direction for the Portuguese empire, his health began to decline soon after his arrival in India. He seemed to work so hard that he exhausted himself. In fact, da Gama had been in India barely three months when he died on Christmas Eve 1524. He was buried at Cochin.

The Empire After Da Gama

Following Dom Vasco's death, his sons—Estêvão and Paulo—left India with a fleet that returned to Portugal early in 1525. Since their father was no longer viceroy, they had lost their important positions in imperial government. Indeed, by the end of the decade, da Gama's policies in India had been changed. The Portuguese began building more forts to protect the pepper trade. Perhaps the most important of these was located on the island of Diu on the northwestern coast in Gujarat.

During the first two decades of the sixteenth century, Diu was governed by Malik Ayaz. According to historian M.N. Pearson, "Under Malik Ayaz's stewardship Diu at 1500 had risen to be one of the great ports of India." It had grown very wealthy on the spice trade and maintained a great deal of independence in Gujarat. The Portuguese wanted to build a factory in Diu, but Ayaz constantly refused. While he was happy to trade with the Portuguese merchants, Ayaz wanted to maintain control of all the wealth that passed through his port. To stop the Portuguese, he had even joined the expedition that defeated Viceroy Almeida's son at Chaul in 1508. Later, in 1513, he refused a request by Governor Albuquerque to put a Portuguese fort in Diu.

Ayaz died in the early 1520s, and a new sultan of Gujarat—Bahadur Shah—decided to strengthen his control of Diu and end its independence. Meanwhile Diu continued to be a thorn in the side of the Portuguese who wanted a monopoly of the pepper trade. Muslim trading ships, avoiding the Portuguese patrols, carried loads of pepper northward from the west coast to Diu. From there they traveled across the Arabian Sea or pepper was carried from Diu by caravan over land into central Asia and westward to the Mediterranean Sea. At first Bahadur Shah was not interested in Portuguese requests to build a fort at Diu, but during the 1520s, a new Muslim empire, the Mogul Empire, had been established at Delhi in central India. The Moguls had defeated Bahadur's armies, and he wanted an alliance with the Portuguese to help defend Gujarat.

As a result, Bahadur Shah gave them permission to build a fort in Diu in 1535. Soon afterward, the sultan realized that he had made a tremendous mistake giving the Portuguese a foothold in Diu. In 1538, Bahadur joined forces with the Ottoman Turks and besieged the Portuguese fort. Although the Portuguese were greatly outnumbered, they held out until a relief force arrived and Bahadur abandoned the siege early in 1539.

A year later, Dom Vasco's son Estêvão da Gama became governor of India. In December 1540, he left Goa with a large fleet of 72 ships headed for the Red Sea. His mission was to destroy a large Ottoman Turkish fleet stationed at Suez at the northern end of the Red Sea. (Egypt had been conquered by the Ottomans several decades earlier.) Over the next several months, da Gama's fleet sailed toward Suez, passing small Egyptian communities along the way. By the end of April, the Portuguese eventually arrived in front of Suez, but it was so heavily guarded by the Turkish fleet that da Gama decided to abandon his mission and return to India. The entire expedition had been a failure.

MAGELLAN

Fernão Magalhaes (Ferdinand Magellan) was a Portuguese explorer, born in Saborosa about 1480. His father, Pedro Ruy de Magalhaes, was a prominent mayor of Saborosa, and Fernão was fortunate enough to be educated in Lisbon at the court of King Manuel. In 1505, he joined Viceroy Francisco de Almeida in his voyage to India and later participated in the Portuguese takeover of Malacca in 1511. During his service in Malacca, however, Magellan disobeyed his commanding officer, left the army, and was discredited in the eyes of King Manuel. Magellan, however, did not lose his interest in voyages of exploration or overseas empire. Nevertheless, he realized that the Portuguese king would not send him on another mission. So he left Portugal and journeyed to Spain, which was developing its own extensive empire in America.

The Spanish also claimed that the Molucca Islands, located east of Malacca, rightfully belonged to them under the Treaty of Tordesillas. Magellan believed that he could reach the Moluccas and claim them for Spain by sailing west through Spanish-held territory rather than east around the Cape of Good Hope, part of the Portuguese trade route. He convinced the Spanish king who agreed to finance his voyage. Magellan's fleet of five ships sailed in September 1519, reaching South America and eventually locating the straits near the southern tip of the continent. Magellan and his crew sailed through these straits into the Pacific Ocean and reached the Philippines in March 1520. There Magellan was killed on the Island of Mactan during a battle with the natives in April.

Nevertheless he had chartered a new route to the Spice Islands of the Far East, and Spain began to develop a lucrative trade in the area.

Da Gama returned to Portugal soon afterward. The new governor, João de Castro, faced a serious crisis in India when Diu was threatened with another attack. This time a small Portuguese force faced a 10,000-man army of Gujaratis, Turks, and Egyptians. The siege began in April 1546, and, as it continued, the garrison was threatened with starvation. They were forced to kill cats and dogs to provide themselves with food. Meanwhile, the Portuguese governor could not relieve the garrison because the strong monsoon winds—common during the spring and summer—prevented his vessels from leaving Goa.

Finally, Castro brought his fleet into Diu in November. Under cover of darkness, men were landed onshore and, using rope ladders, climbed into the fortress. To keep the Muslims from learning what was going on, "a flotilla of small boats, with lights ablaze, trumpets sounding and a forest of lances bristling on deck, was rowed to and fro by non-combatants [nonsoldiers] so as to distract attention from the landing parties," according to K. G. Jayne.

Once inside the fortress, Governor Castro and his military advisers began to develop a plan. Their ships would sail in one direction trying to convince the Muslims that they were going to land about a mile from the fortress. Meanwhile, the troops inside would launch an attack on the Muslim siege lines. The plan worked, and about 3,000 of the Muslim soldiers including their leader, Rumi Khan, were killed, saving Diu.

While the Portuguese were successful in defending their empire against the Muslims, later in the sixteenth century, they faced new problems. In 1580, Portugal was conquered by Spain. The Spanish had their own enormous empire in America, and also claimed part of the Portuguese possessions in the East Indies. The Spanish were far more interested in defending their own colonies than in spending money on the Portuguese empire in India.

Da Gama's legacy in India includes the territories of Daman, Salsette, Bombay, Baçaim, Diu, and Goa. These settlements made up Portuguese India, with Goa serving as its headquarters. The Portuguese continued to have a major presence in India until 1960, influencing its politics, religion, and trade. Pictured is a Portuguese fort in Goa.

The Portuguese had always been forced to deal with a shortage in manpower. There were never enough men to adequately garrison all the forts or provide crews for all the ships that were necessary to defend the empire. Portugal had also failed to develop a large merchant class. The king wanted a monopoly of the spice trade and did not encourage independent merchants to participate in it. As a result, the spices were sold for gold and silver to merchants from other parts of Europe, especially the English and the Dutch. But, as K.G. Jayne pointed out, "it was unlikely that they would long remain mere agents," buying spices for gold and silver. "In due time they would fit out their own vessels, import and sell on their own behalf. By undertaking the whole venture of Indian traffic they could reduce expenses and double profits."

Goa was a highly profitable trading port until the end of the sixteenth century, but by this time Dutch warships had appeared. Over the next half century, they defeated the Portuguese and gradually took control of most of their forts and factories. From 1629 to 1635, for example, 1,500 Portuguese men were killed and they had lost 155 ships. Gradually, their empire began to disappear. From over 50 forts, they had only 9 by 1666, including Goa, Diu, and Chaul.

Meanwhile, the Portuguese had decided to spend more time and money on their colony in Brazil. Pedro Cabral had landed there in the early sixteenth century before traveling to India. During the seventeenth century, the Portuguese developed lucrative sugarcane plantations in Brazil. They imported thousands of slaves from Africa to work the plantations. Sugar mills expanded from 60 in 1570 to 300 in 1645, processing the sugarcane and sending shiploads of sugar to Europe. Many Portuguese went to Brazil to start plantations and share in the wealth to be made from sugar. While Brazil had a population of 25,000 settlers in 1600, only about 2,000 Portuguese lived in Goa.

While interest in Brazil increased, the Portuguese focus on India declined. The empire that da Gama had hoped to establish proved to be only short-lived. His expeditions to India had opened up new trade routes and revolutionized the economy of Europe. But the Portuguese lacked the manpower, the money, and the interest to hold onto most of their colonies. They were gradually lost to other European powers.

CHRONOLOGY

1394	Henry the Navigator born in Portugal.
1415	Portuguese capture Ceuta in North Africa.
1424	Portuguese invade Canary Islands.
	Henry's explorers reach Cape Bojador in West Africa.
1438	Afonso V becomes king of Portugal.
	Slaves are imported from Africa to Portugal.

TIMELINE

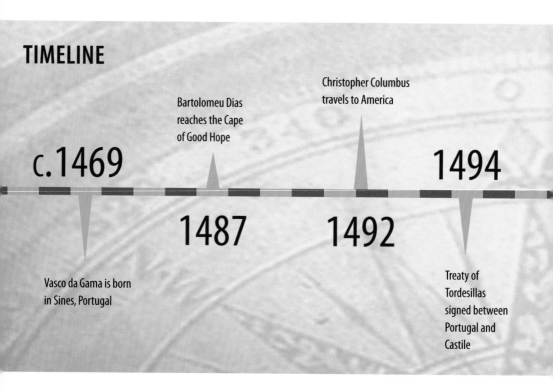

Bartolomeu Dias reaches the Cape of Good Hope

Christopher Columbus travels to America

c.1469

1494

1487

1492

Vasco da Gama is born in Sines, Portugal

Treaty of Tordesillas signed between Portugal and Castile

1456	Henry's explorers reach the Gambia River.
1460	Prince Henry dies.
c. 1469	Vasco da Gama is born in Sines, Portugal.
1481	Portuguese establish Elmina on West African coast.
	John II becomes king of Portugal.
1487	Bartolomeu Dias reaches the Cape of Good Hope.
1492	Christopher Columbus travels to America.
1494	Treaty of Tordesillas signed between Portugal and Castile.
1498	Vasco da Gama arrives in Calicut, India.
1500	Pedro Cabral travels to Brazil, then India.

Da Gama
arrives in
Calicut, India

Da Gama makes
a second voyage
to India

Da Gama dies
in Cochin

1500

1510

1498

1502

1524

Pedro Cabral travels to
Brazil, then India

1510–1515
Albuquerque establishes
Portuguese empire

1502	Da Gama makes a second voyage to India.
1505	Francisco de Almeida becomes viceroy of India.
1509	Afonso de Albuquerque becomes governor of India.
1510–1515	Albuquerque establishes Portuguese empire.
1515	Albuquerque dies.
1521	John III becomes king of Portugal.
1524	Da Gama appointed viceroy of India; dies in Cochin.

GLOSSARY

ALIDADE   a metal pointer on an astrolabe

ASTROLABE   a navigational device used to determine latitude

CAFILA   convoy of merchant ships protected by Portuguese armed vessels

CARAVEL   a small three-masted sailing ship with lateen sails

CARTAZ   special pass issued by the Portuguese in India permitting a merchant ship to carry on trade

CROSSBOW   mechanical device used to shoot arrows

FATHOM   a nautical measurement equaling six feet

IBERIA   peninsula in western Europe where Spain and Portugal are located

INDIGO   a purple dye used by royalty in Europe to color their garments

ISLAM   religion founded by the Prophet Muhammad in the eighth century

KNOT   nautical speed of about one mile per hour

LATEEN SAIL   a triangular sail

LEAGUE   a measurement at sea equaling about 250 miles

MUSLIM   a follower of Islam

RESIN   liquid substance produced by a tree

SCRIVENER   a member of a ship's crew who kept a record of the voyage and an accounting of the trade being conducted

SCURVY   a disease caused by lack of Vitamin C that can be fatal

VICEROY   supreme governor in India

ZAMORIN   a Hindu prince who ruled an Indian state

BIBLIOGRAPHY

Birmingham, David. *A Concise History of Portugal*. New York: Cambridge University Press, 2003.

Boxer, R.R. *The Portuguese Seaborne Empire, 1415-1825*. New York: Knopf, 1969.

Jayne, K.G. *Vasco de Gama and His Successors, 1460-1580*. New York: Barnes and Noble, 1970.

Koestler-Grack, Rachel. *Vasco da Gama and the Sea Route to India*. New York: Chelsea House Publishers, 2005.

Pearson, M.N. *The Portuguese in India*. New York: Cambridge University Press, 1987.

Russell, Peter. *Prince Henry "the Navigator" A Life*. New Haven, CT: Yale University Press, 2000.

Subrahmanyam, Sanjay. *The Career and Legend of Vasco Da Gama*. New York: Cambridge University Press, 2002.

Turner, Jack. *Spice: The History of a Temptation*. New York: Knopf, 2004.

FURTHER RESOURCES

Calvert, Patricia. *Vasco da Gama: So Strong a Spirit*. Tarrytown, N.Y.: Benchmark Books, 2005.

Crompton, Samuel Willard. *Robert de la Salle*. New York: Chelsea House, 2009.

Doak, Robin. *Da Gama: Vasco da Gama Sails Around the Cape of Good Hope*. Mankato, Minn.: Compass Point Books, 2002.

Koestler-Grack, Rachel A. *Ferdinand Magellan*. New York: Chelsea House, 2009.

Lace, William W. *Captain James Cook*. New York: Chelsea House, 2009.

———. *Sir Francis Drake*. New York: Chelsea House, 2009.

Larkin, Tanya. *Vasco da Gama*. New York: PowerKids Press, 2001.

WEB SITES

The European Voyages of Exploration: The Sea-Route to India and Vasco da Gama
http://www.ucalgary.ca/applied_history/tutor/eurvoya/vasco.html
Detailed information about voyages of European explorers in the fifteenth and sixteenth centuries.

Modern History Sourcebook: Vasco da Gama: Round Africa to India, 1497–1498
http://www.fordham.edu/halsall/mod/1497degama.html
A listing of thousands of sources for research on ancient, medieval, and modern history.

The Western and Central Chronology (WebChron): Vasco da Gama Arrives in India
http://www.thenagain.info/WebChron/WestEurope/DaGama.html
Chronologies developed by instructors and students intended for use in history classes.

PICTURE CREDITS

INDEX

ABOUT
THE AUTHOR

RICHARD WORTH holds a B.A. and an M.A. in colonial American history from Trinity College in Connecticut. He currently teaches writing to third and fourth graders. Worth has published more than 50 books on biography, history, current events, and the criminal justice system. His book *Gangs and Crime* from Chelsea House was included on the New York Public Library's Best Books for the Teen Age list.